The Economics of
Being a Woman

The Economics of Being a Woman

Dee Dee Anern
with Betsy Bliss

McGraw-Hill Book Company

New York · St. Louis · San Francisco · Bogota · Düsseldorf
Madrid · Mexico · Montreal · Panama · Paris
São Paulo · Tokyo · Toronto

Reprinted by arrangement with
Macmillan Publishing Co., Inc.

First McGraw-Hill Paperback edition, 1977

67890 FGRFGR 83210

Library of Congress Cataloging in Publication Data

Ahern, Dee Dee.
  The economics of being a woman.

  Originally published by Macmillan, New York.
  Includes bibliographical references and indexes.
  1. Women—United States—Economic conditions. 2. Finance, Personal. I. Bliss, Betsy, joint author. II. Title.
[HQ1426.A35   1977]   332'.02'4   77-24735
ISBN 0-07-00650-4

To Josephine Kelleher,

my grandmother, a woman rich in love and wisdom,
but who died lonely, because she was poor.

Contents

Contents

Introduction

How do you measure the wisdom and experience a woman gathers throughout her lifetime? . . . With this wisdom she molds society through its children, its families, its communities, its schools, and the business world.

But how can she measure her economic status in return?

THIS IS A book that could touch the life of every woman, because it is about the economic factors, risks, and obstacles that shape her life.

It examines the personal economic life of the American woman from three perspectives: *the past*—the customs, laws, and economic history that lie at the root of her current complex economic concerns; *the present*—a measure of her economic contributions to family, community, business, and government, with a graphic view of the money sources and systems that direct and control her personal economic life; and *the future*—providing a framework for viewing human life value in economic terms that will allow women to participate fully with men in the economic growth and security of their families, communities, and country.

It also analyzes the legal pickpocketing of each woman's paycheck and the high price the American woman and her family have paid for this economic exploitation.

It will probably outrage government, business, and insurance leaders who, over the years, have relied on and profited from the untapped pools of women's resources and fringe benefits, and who have enjoyed this good fortune thanks to women's historic naivete and unfamiliarity with lifetime financial planning.

We women have allowed this erosion of our livelihoods under the illusion that we have been making economic choices. Because we have been able to make consumer choices that affect our life-styles, we have thought we've had control over our economic destinies. But upon closer scrutiny, we see that most of the important economic choices have already been made for us—leaving men and women alike with "no-win" alternatives.

Financial awareness among women is growing at a pace unprecedented in our history; one might even consider it a financial revolution.

Looking back over the last eight years, during which time I've been researching the financial and economic life of women, it seems more like a miracle than a revolution. In 1968, few (men or women) were willing to discuss the subject, and their knowledge and awareness of the problem were extremely limited. Research material and resource people were difficult to find.

In the subsequent eight years statistics and awareness have been mounting at a staggering rate.

This book, therefore, could not have been written or understood until now. It is the first of its kind to take a "total picture" approach in examining women's total contributions to the American economy—and the disproportionate benefits they and their families receive from a system whose laws and mores are geared to the life- and work-styles of men.

An individual's search for a personal, lifetime financial strategy is all too often frustrating because it is fragmented; the economics of marketing financial education makes it unprofitable for bankers, brokers, insurance agents, lawyers, and accountants to take the time to do lifetime planning with anyone but one whose wealth justifies the effort. Moreover, each specialist has his own ax to grind.

My research differs from most because its purpose was not to determine the marketing potential of a particular product, and it was not commissioned or funded by a foundation, corporation, university, or government agency. Defying all the rules of sound money management (and with the cooperation of my oldest son, who agreed to put himself through college and law school), I funded it myself.

I became interested in the financial and economic lives of women when I was in the insurance industry. Working with families in hundreds of homes, I found that many women were not only uncomfortable discussing financial matters but had little knowledge of the financial factors that controlled and directed their economic lives.

However, the real tragedy of our lack of choice in controlling our own economic destinies became evident when I started working with senior citizens who had "budgeted and saved" all their lives, who had followed the rules of "sound financial planning," and yet found themselves destitute toward the end of their lives. Their hopelessness and bewilderment at what they had "done wrong" convinced me of the need to take a new look at the systems controlling our economic lives and to find new ways to regain control over our economic self-determination.

Realizing that the complexity and seriousness of these economic problems would continue to grow and not diminish, I began researching *the impact of women and their money sources on society and the economy.*

I have crisscrossed this nation many times in the last eight years interviewing executives of financial institutions; business, professional, and government leaders; educators; and women themselves. Most of my research was done in Los Angeles, San Francisco, New York, Washington, D.C., and Chicago, and throughout the states of California and Illinois, from the smallest hamlets to the largest cities.

I hear daily testimony of women's economic concerns from the 300 to 1,000 women who attend my Money Manager

Workshops and lectures each month. I conduct these economic education workshops for universities, banks, and business and civic groups throughout the country.

To understand fully women's role in the economy, one must search for answers far beyond business, finance, and economics—in law, social science, psychology, political science, anthropology, religions, cultures, philosophy, history, medicine, biology, labor relations, communications, technology, media, art, literature, national and international politics, and education.

No one person could possibly research and interpret all the necessary sciences, arts, and disciplines, but perhaps in time the economic influences of each will be examined.

If we are to enjoy economic growth, an economy not based on consumption and conflict, then we must learn to maximize the human and economic resources of every American, man and woman, and to develop new concepts, tools, techniques—and new choices.

I am pleased to share with you some of my findings, suggestions, and alternative choices.

—DEE DEE AHERN

PART I

The Unmeasured: Women's Economic Lives

•••➤◉◆◉➤•••

CHAPTER 1

Women's Economics: Is There a Difference?

Woman, if rated by the scant attention she gets in American historical writing, is the forgotten sex. . . . The omission of woman from American chronicles is an indictment of the civilization itself, evidence of an unbalanced appraisal of events and values.

—ERNEST R. GROVES
*The American Woman: The
Feminine Side of a Masculine
Civilization*[1]

"WOMEN'S ECONOMICS, what's *that*?" I've been asked this question almost daily for the past eight years, and each time the query is accompanied by a furrowed brow, a wrinkled nose, a quizzical look.

The economics of being a woman and of being a man are so vastly different that it is shocking to realize that few in our educated and affluent society recognize or understand the distinction.

Women's economic research, moreover, is virtually an unexplored field. Because of this, neither experts nor women themselves appreciate the many subtle ways women are the primary victims of our economic system. As individuals, wo-

1

men have completely different economic concerns and obstacles than men. As a group, women are a major economic force in the nation's production and consumption, yet their contributions are neither adequately counted nor rewarded.

Instead, government officials, businessmen, and economists parrot popular mythology which devalues women's labor and assumes that women should be dependent and therefore need "protection."

(Selling this need for "protection" has become big business. Women's dependency has meant high cost for individual women and their families and high profit for the corporate and government "protectors.")

Our collective myopia about women's economics springs partly from our social "wisdom," which reserves for men the "more basic and important economic role," providing financial security: acquiring, accumulating, conserving, and distributing wealth. From childhood, a man is programmed for a life of financial responsibility. It is interwoven with his self-image and success image. Early in life a man lays the groundwork for his business and professional goals. In fact, for generations sons gained their economic status directly, as apprentices with their fathers, learning their skills or trades as young men. Until the fifteenth or sixteenth century, this hereditary allocation of tasks was considered a main stabilizing force within society.[2]

In contrast, women perform the functions of consumption and household management: selection, processing, and administration of family goods and services (functions with no economic value in our present value system). From childhood women are trained by their mothers for lives in the home. They are taught that their roles are supportive and subject to the needs and desires of their families. For generations, daughters have gained their economic status indirectly, either from their fathers or husbands. Even today, the economic security of women is more a matter of chance than choice.

Our short-sightedness about women's economics also reflects the way statistics are compiled. Numerical measures universally fail to count women's unpaid contributions to the economic well-being of the nation, in their roles as homemakers and mothers, and as participants and volunteers contributing to the economic growth of civic and community life.

John Kenneth Galbraith gives us some insight into homemakers' unmeasured economic roles. As he states in his *Economics and the Public Purpose*:

"The value of the services of housewives has been calculated at roughly one-fourth of the total Gross National Product. However, the labor of women to facilitate consumption is not valued in the national income or product. This is of some importance for its disguise: *what is not counted is not often noticed* [italics added]. For this reason, it becomes possible for women to study economics without becoming aware of their precise role in the economy."[3]

(Along these lines, I find it interesting that the work of a maid or housekeeper is counted in the Gross National Product, but if the maid or housekeeper marries her employer, she is no longer counted.)

Statistics do count women's presence in the labor market—but they only count part of women's contributions. For many years, the Department of Labor has meticulously chronicled the demographics of female employees, but neither the department nor anyone else has computed women's contributions into the economy and society through their weekly deposits from *the other side of their paychecks*, the side where deductions are taken out of gross income for fringe benefits, pensions, and Social Security.

Some 40 to 50 percent of each woman's paycheck is automatically removed and deposited into the three major reservoirs of money that substantially fund our entire economic system: into government revenues through taxation (Social Security, city, state, and federal taxes); into insurance companies through her fringe benefit deposits (premiums); and into insurance, banking, and investment companies, through her deposit into pension pools.

These deposits are made in her name supposedly for her and her family's future benefit, but she has found historically (and statistics validate) that she and her family will receive little or no benefit from these hard-earned deposits because of the fine-print loopholes of regulations, requirements, limitations, and qualifications. Even though the average woman worker will spend twenty-five years in the labor force, she finds herself penalized because of her mobility and stop-start work patterns due to family responsibilities; her duplication of benefits through her spouse; and her low wage base.

In effect, the nation's 37.7 million working women have been major funding agents for Social Security, welfare, and government revenues, as well as the pension and insurance industries, by accepting low or nonexistent returns on their costly deposits.

The ironic twist to this tale is its "magic" ending. Once half a woman's paycheck is contributed to these benefit pools, these monies are transformed from "her" money into "their" money by our subtle transfer payment system. The woman is told that *if she qualifies* she will be getting "protection" and "something for nothing," as though it were a matter of government and corporate largesse rather than her rightful collection of her benefits from her deposit. As we shall see in later chapters, the real cost of "protection" and "getting something for nothing" is high indeed. The ultimate victims of a woman's economic exploitation are her beneficiaries—her spouse, her children, her loved ones.

Why do women and their families put up with this "paycheck leakage" that drains away permanently up to half a woman's earnings? One answer lies in the different ways women and their spouses view their productive roles. Until this generation, men considered working wives an insult to their masculine, breadwinner image. A wife in the job force was apologized for and explained away with "She wants a dishwasher," or "She needs to get away from the kids," etc. Women in turn echoed their spouses' attitudes and regarded their own work as temporary; they never stopped to evaluate what benefits their contributions would bring. Even though 58 percent of the women in the work force are married, many of them still can't bring themselves to admit they intend to work for a lifetime. And such an admission by a single woman has until now been tantamount to an acknowledgment of spinsterhood.

But all this is changing, and swiftly—almost faster than business and government can absorb. The impact of women and their money sources on society and the economy is being put under the microscope and scrutinized by women, issue by issue. Women's examination of credit, Social Security, pensions, and insurance has brought major changes in business practices and laws. Women collectively are educating themselves about the mechanics of money and are sharing their common feelings and problems. This new awareness, knowledge, and investigation will continue to bring changes at all levels of government, business, and education.

Whether her deposit is in *time, money, or ability,* today's woman realizes she is contributing substantially to the family, home, community, government, and business world. She wants to know what benefits she's getting from these deposits—*for the numbers don't add up.* She's changing the terms of the age-old bargain which

- Placed no value on her household management and community contributions,
- Undervalued her employment in the labor force,
- Exploited her deposits from the *other side of her paycheck,*
- Limited her access to ownership, contracts, property and inheritance.

She is standing up to be counted

The economics of being a woman means recognizing that you have an economic life that can be charted and measured. It means looking at the total picture of your economic lifetime—and anticipating and planning for the various changes and crises that may occur gradually or instantly by

Aging
Childbirth
Marriage
Divorce
Illness
Dependents
Remarriage
Widowhood
Unemployment
Education
Retirement
Entering or re-entering the labor market . . . and many other factors.

CHAPTER 2

Society of Enemies—or Partners?

The feminine role in the birth of the nation cries out for formulation and affirmation. The *mater familias* is unfamiliar to the pages of old school American historians. We require a declaration of independence for historiography in which women shall have their place. In interpretation of the American past, woman has been subject to a *conspiracy of silence.* . . .

—WALTER HUNT BLUMENTHAL
American Panorama[1]

THROUGH ALL OF HISTORY, women have contributed substantially to the home and community. Theirs, however, has been a silent history, seldom chronicled in the archives.

The cooperation and work of both men and women were vital to the success of the home and state.

In an agricultural society in which man's and woman's life and labor were interwoven and centered in the home, where the home was the focus of employment, trade, and education, woman's contribution was visible and crucial, even though not recorded, measured, or paid for.

However, as the industrial society separated man and woman from their joint effort in the home, a new economic pattern and value system began.

The art of household management was a key factor in the first written economic study of society, Aristotle's *oikonomia* (from whence the name economics was derived). He was the first to question, "What is value?" "What is the basis of exchange?" "What is interest?"[2] He differentiated economics into two branches: housecraft (use) and statecraft (gain); not production and consumption, as we have done.

By housecraft he meant the art of household management, the careful use of resources. Statecraft was the use of nature's resources and of human skills for acquisitive purposes, economic activity that had as its motive and end not use, but profit.

As statecraft (work for profit) became more dominant and important to man's economic survival, and as his work took place primarily outside the home, rather than in it, the measured value of housecraft disappeared.

Housecraft was, in fact, the foundation of the colonization of our country. The combined efforts of men, women, and children were necessary in a new, developing nation where resources were abundant and labor and money scarce.

With large families an important economic asset, woman's role in the increase in population was obviously of great importance. The magnitude of this increase was noted by Ben Franklin in 1755: "There were near a million souls in the colonies, though only some 80,000 had been brought over by sea."

Our country had its roots in economic motives. The families that built our country were poor; one of England's purposes in colonization was to furnish an outlet for her surplus population.[3] In the mother country, unemployment was widespread; the demand for labor had declined; and the cessation of the European wars left many men without income or profession.

In addition, inflation was rampant; by 1640, money in Europe had sunk to about one-fifth of its former value. The colonies also served England as a source of raw materials and a new market for the home country's products.

Many colonists came to America as indentured servants, convicts, and slaves. The voluntary indentured servants had no money—and had their passage and maintenance guaranteed in return for a period of service. The involuntary indentured servants were convicts, sentenced to servitude in the colonies for offenses ranging from vagrancy to debt to crime.

All these newcomers to the New World were spurred by hopes of economic opportunity, but only the hardiest of families could withstand the hardships and poverty of life in pioneer settlements.

The industrious women of colonial America managed their (often isolated) homes as nearly self-sufficient enterprises.

As the colonial population grew, and villages and towns sprang up, a different kind of household economy developed —"cottage industry," independent households organized to produce goods at home for sale in the marketplace. In these cottage businesses family members worked together, producing such goods as linen, lace, and knit fabrics, to bring in extra income. It was common for mothers to read stories and lessons aloud while the rest of the family worked at the loom or workbench.

Meanwhile, the Industrial Revolution sweeping through Europe took hold in America, and workshops and factories began to replace home industry. Women left their looms at home for looms at the plant. Machines moved the center of production from the fireside to the factory—and in the process, the marketplace replaced the home as society's basic economic institution. Families no longer produced for their own use and gain, but sold their labor to others in return for money.

The tradition of paying low wages to women began when the factory overtook the home as the principal site of earning a livelihood. Men in the labor force were paid so little that their families had to continue cottage industry to get by. Manufacturers paid women and children a pittance for home production—and found this subcontracting system advantageous, because the various subcontractors could not compare their pay. Women accepted pitiful wages out of need and ignorance.

Industrialization wrought another, even more profound, change in family economics. The pull of the factory removed

men from their dominant role in housecraft. Industrial man
no longer saw control of his economic destiny, his success,
even his "manliness," as centered in the home with interdependent family members.

He became a link in a new chain of dependency; his family
became dependent on him, and he became dependent on business, and, to a lesser extent, government.

When man left the home, the home lost its economic value.
Today, according to Scott Burns in *Home, Inc*: "Economists
barely recognize that it [the household] exists, caring little
beyond that it consume an adequate number of dishwashers
and continue to save at the appropriate rate."[4] Moreover, the
transformation that took men out of the home, Burns continues, "left women in charge of an institution that no longer
served a clear and overtly valued economic purpose.

*"The household became a 'cost center' rather than a 'profit
center' and all those associated with it, mainly women, lost
status, power, and self-esteem* [italics added]."[5]

The waxing of industrial society and the waning of agri-
culture and cottage industry also brought a whole new definition of "the virtuous woman." While women in earlier
societies were valued for their procreative capacities and
productive energies, industrialization pushed women into the
leftover role of administering to a now-dependent institution.

This "new" virtuous woman was praised for her household management, but it was a different kind of household
management than had existed previously. The colonial art of
housecraft had been based on production for one's own use;
the "new" household management was based on consumption
of the goods produced in the factory. "In consequence," says
Galbraith, "a new social virtue came to attach to . . . in-
telligent shopping for goods, their preparation . . . and care
and maintenance of the dwelling and other possessions. . . .
Social life became in large measure a display of virtuosity in
the performance of these functions."[6] The once-independent

household was recast as dependent, and the major instrument for consumption.

As our economic patterns and value systems changed, our economic security no longer came from the natural growth of human and agricultural resources.

Our new economic value system interpreted economics in terms of division—how will the pie be divided?

Economic growth by its natural definition means to multiply, not divide—to create growth rather than divide it.

A society of enemies began when we went from providing for each other to profiting from each other.

The transformation from a household economy to a marketing economy, Scott Burns noted, "has brought with it for over a century an ever mounting conflict between the sexes that is now seen as direct competition for jobs, salaries, the power and self-esteem attached to productive work."[7]

Women's productive role became a threat, and only her consumptive role became important to this new economy.

The perceptive Charlotte Perkins Gilman capsuled this new economic value system in her extraordinary and prophetic *Women and Economics* written in 1898: "Our difficulty about wealth is not in getting it out of the earth, but in getting it away from each other."[8]

We now have a society of enemies, with women and men against each other, women and women against each other, people and government against each other, the worker and business against each other, the rich and the poor against each other—and now we have the young and old against each other. The old are told they must retire to make room for the young—and the young are told they must pay exorbitant taxes to provide security for the old.

The growth of our subtle transfer payment system has created new burdens of responsibility and guilt, and a new target for hostility.

This was reflected in an interview during a recent trip to

Washington to update this book's statistics and investigate pending legislation affecting women. An attorney for a major Capitol Hill committee questioned, "If working wives don't make excess deposits to overlapping health insurance benefits, who will make up the profit for the insurance industry?"

Another question often asked is, "If working wives don't deposit 11.7 percent of their income into Social Security for little or no benefit, who will make up the difference?"

Our economic lives are no longer determined solely by individual and family decisions.

Our responsibility to, our mandatory contributions to, and our predetermined benefits from the major money pools of government, business, and insurance have made our economic future and quality of life dependent on our role in the collective society.

To understand women's economic role in this society, we must understand and analyze the systems and laws that determine the benefits they will receive from the deposits they make.

Women want to be partners in our society, not enemies.

CHAPTER 3

1 + 1 = ½ = Dependency

Any human being that by nature belongs not to himself but to another is by nature a slave. . . .

—ARISTOTLE
Politics[1]

THE DICTIONARY DEFINES DEPENDENT AS: "The state of depending on or needing someone or something for aid, support or the like; subordination or subjection; to be suspended, undetermined or pending."

In every age including our own the economics of being a woman has been intimately tied to dependency.

But what is dependency? It is a word bantered around a lot these days. Its shades of meaning divide modern women and their families. Its supposed antonym, independence, also carries many meanings and, unfortunately, also fuels divisiveness.

Independence is a word footballed around as though it were a state of being that threatens the family; women's independence, we read, is responsible for today's high divorce rate.

In like manner, dependency is praised as a virtue, the holy attribute of good wives and mothers.

And, at the same time, independence has acquired combative overtones. It is seen as the opposite of cooperation, which is mistakenly identified with submission.

This semantic battle completely confuses the real issues. The brouhaha over dependence-independence blinds us to the mutual strength and growth we gain through independence and interdependence. It obscures, too, the economic waste, risk, and vulnerability that go hand in hand with dependency.

Dependency means that one plus one equals one-half. The age-old customs, attitudes, and archaic laws persisting even today that build dependency into our relationships with our families and into our relationships with business and government make each of us split economic personalities. Our chains of dependency bind families in such a way that our economic value is divided in half—rather than multiplied by the joint efforts of two independent people building an economic life together.

To understand the problems of dependency today, we must seek its root causes by going back to history.

Where did dependency begin? It is interwoven in our religions, cultures, customs, laws, and traditions from the most primitive times. Throughout history women have been valued variously as property, as cheap labor, and as child bearers.

The tradition of women as property dates from the earliest tribes when women were a kind of currency, traded in exchange for cattle and land.[2] The great economic theorist Thorstein Veblen once said he believed the whole institution of ownership began with the ownership of women. Even today in some cultures, the custom of the dowry continues to place a money value on women.

Though putting a price tag on a woman is now considered inhumane, the ancient idea of women as symbols of their husbands' wealth and prestige carries on, though in more subtle and sophisticated forms. Tribal warriors fought battles with women as the prizes of triumph. The most successful warrior was the one who possessed not only the most beautiful and desirable female captives, but also the most industrious. Many women producing many goods were signs of status.

Today's marriage market puts little premium on women's

industry—since modern machines do much of women's house-
work, and the factory has replaced the home as the center of
production for family goods. But the marital marketplace continues the tradition of prestige connected with owning a beautiful wife.

Today, Thomas Wiseman's *The Money Motive* notes with
tongue in cheek: "Those that are the most bedworthy *looking*
go to the highest bidder. The fact that these often turn out to
be unbedable . . . is neither here nor there. Their main purpose
is to be living proofs of the fact that their husbands can
afford them, and, therefore, by sophistic deduction, are great
men."[3]

The tradition of women as property was enforced by the
tools of laws and customs.

From our Judaic-Christian past came the custom of patriarchy—the male, either father or eldest son, as head of the
family. Property belonged to the patriarch; all the wives and
children and servants were under his dominion.

Patriarchy was codified into law as primogeniture, which
gave first-born sons inheritance rights over all other males;
female offspring had no inheritance rights.

As late as the founding of this country, women were regarded as having no legal existence separate from that of their
husbands. Upon marriage, a wife's property was surrendered
to the ownership and control of her spouse.

Walter Hunt Blumenthal's *American Panorama* notes: "Although wisdom prevailed among the Founding Fathers, when
the Declaration [of Independence] said all men are created
equal, it consciously overlooked women. This was because
the Blackstone legal tradition designating women as marital
appanages of men was in full sway. It was only later American
commentators on law and equity . . . qualified the common
law doctrine expounded by Blackstone that husband and
liege wife are 'one person.' "

It was 15 years after 1776 before various states abolished

primogeniture and provided for the equality of inheritance among all children. And it was a full 150 years later that women gained equal citizenship, in the form of the right to vote— "thereby extending to women," Blumenthal added, "the realization of one of those human values implicit in the Declaration but not proclaimed in it."[4]

Customs and laws also fostered women's dependency due to their biological roles as child bearers. And, though the economic value of children has changed dramatically over the ages, the dependency tradition has not.

Natural fertility, not hindered by contraception, meant that most women spent most of their child-bearing years pregnant. Moreover, as infant mortality was very high, a woman had to bear many children in order to have a sufficient number hardy enough to survive stillbirths and infant diseases.

Originally, children were necessary because they contributed to the family welfare. But later the high cost of each child made it impossible for most couples to afford large families. Charlotte Perkins Gilman explained how this change came about: "In simple early times there was a period when women were economically profited by child-bearing; when, indeed, that was their sole use, and, failing it, they were entitled to no respect or profit whatever." When economic activity was centered in the home, children were extra, unpaid hands. Thus, the more children, the better.

But, Gilman continues, "With industrial development and the increasing weight of economic cares upon the shoulders of the man, children come to be looked upon as a burden, and are dreaded instead of desired by the hardworked father."[5]

The speed with which family planning has taken hold in this country can be seen from a *Wall Street Journal* article on the future of the family. In 1900 the average American family had five children; today the average is 2.3 children.[6] (The 1976 figures show the average is now 1.8 children.)

A fellow suffragette of Gilman's, Frances Squires Potter, in *Women, Economics and the Ballot* further argued that "when women became property, it was inevitable that she should exaggerate her sex. It was that function largely which gave her her value to man." While, Potter said, prostitution is no longer openly tolerated, "public opinion does not yet castigate the parent who makes business success the test of a suitor's desirability. . . . The girl now uses her sex as the utilitarian politician does his vote. She makes a permanent investment. Her sex is a business asset."

Thus, by tradition and law, women have come to gain their economic status indirectly from the success of the men to whom they belong.

Potter added: "The reason women are cheaper than men is because they are more helpless. The reason children are cheaper than women is because they are still more helpless."[7]

While waiting to be interviewed on a recent television show, on which Masters and Johnson were also guests, Dr. Virginia Johnson and I were discussing the impact of money on the sexual relationship. She gave me an excellent comparative analysis: "As long as we have a double standard in money just as we have in sex—in money matters man is the provider, woman is the dependent; in sex matters man has the right, woman has the duty—these problems will continue to be interrelated. We need a committed and sharing relationship in both."[8]

In affairs erotic and economic, men are supposed to *do* and women are supposed to be *done to*. The man is the active, responsible, dominant partner. The woman is passive—and dependent in the dictionary sense: subordinated, suspended.

This economic double standard holds as much power over our family lives as it did in the days when people married for property, not for love. And it persists at the same time that our sexual revolution is teaching couples that men and women have equal sexual rights, responsibilities, and obligations— that partners as independent persons make for a fuller, growing sexual and emotional relationship.

It must be confusing to the minds of children to see this

double standard in operation. From their mothers they learn values and set their goals of self-confidence and self-reliance. Yet in their mothers they see the practice of dependence. Her duties as a mother and her duties as the economic subordinate are in conflict, and can only lead to children's turmoil as they mature. Having learned from their mothers the goal of independence, they could grow to dislike and disrespect her for her own weakness.

The double standard skews women's assumptions about their economic roles as well as society's views of the economics of being a woman.

Our girlish dreams that call for a white knight who will care and provide for us are a fantasy. White knights are practically extinct. In reality, chances are that a young girl will take a husband not only for better or worse, but more or less in debt. And in these days of multiple marriages, a woman can't count on a lifetime allowance any more than she can bank on finding a man not already loaded down with alimony and child-support payments from his previous trips to the altar. In these inflationary times, moreover, few families can afford to have only one breadwinner.

Our laws and customs still operate under the presumption that a woman will be married to one man for the rest of her life and can be dependent on him for her lifetime. This assumption is in direct contrast to the realities of our everyday lives, which show that today's women are not and cannot be dependent on a man:

- 455 out of every 1,000 marriages end in divorce.
- There are 10 million widows in this country.
- The incidence of divorce has increased 166 percent since 1950 and the incidence of widowhood has increased 40 percent since 1950.
- 70 percent of all divorced persons will remarry.
- 58 percent of the nation's wives work and contribute

some 25 to 40 percent of their families' incomes. Some 16 percent of the women in the work force have husbands earning under $7,000 a year.

• 42 percent of working women are single, widowed, or divorced—with no man to depend on.

Dependency today forms a more complex web affecting our economic lives, because we are not only dependent as individuals, but are dependent as groups and a society.

Women's and children's dependency on men forms only a part of the chain of dependency that binds our lives. As families our economic independence is also circumscribed by business and government. As industrialization took man out of the home and put him in the factory, he became dependent on business, and more indirectly, government, for his economic livelihood. He became part of a chain of dependency that began with the helpless child who was dependent on the mother who was dependent on the husband who was dependent on the larger institutions of society that wielded the tools to control his money sources.

The hegemony of the state gradually transformed many of the functions of the family into functions of the state, making the family more and more dependent on forces outside its control. Today government has taken over the challenge of providing social cohesion. It has taken on the functions of educating, caring for the sick and old, equalizing opportunities, and maintaining incomes. The cost of this dependency affects not only each of us but the costs of society as a whole.

Our modern revulsion at the cost of government is not only a logical objection to the high costs of government service but also an expression of *our rage against dependency.*

Today we live in a system in which dependency is an economic disadvantage, and yet all our laws assume its existence and promote it. The problem of dependency is that it offers no protection. He who is dependent is vulnerable to crisis

changes and to others' control—and is often without resources
to cope with them.

The problem of dependency is the economic waste and risk
it entails. Despite its centuries-old hold on us, dependency
has not built a better world.

The new women emerging at the end of this century are
not dependent. Statistics show their increasing education, increasing role in the job market, increasing economic responsibility. They recognize that family strength and growth is
obtained through the cooperation and joint efforts of economic independents—that women's independence is a boon
rather than a threat to family life.

Just as the death of the double standard in sex has removed
the heavy burden of "performance" from the man and replaced it with responsibility, commitment, and mutual respect
for human worth in intimate relations, the death of the double
standard in money will help, not hinder, men.

As wives begin to share more of a family's financial burdens, "men will be able to relax, and that could ease tensions
in the family," according to Lyle Slaughter, Director of
Counselling at the San Francisco Family Service, quoted in
the *Wall Street Journal.* Margaret Mead echoed these senti-
ments in the same article: "Nobody looks at father and thinks
what a life he'd have if he hadn't those five children. He might
have been able to paint instead of being a stockbroker. Or
[be] a musician instead of running a jewelry store he inherited."[9]

Women, who began the twentieth century with winning
political independence, will end this century with economic
independence. They are rebelling against archaic laws and
customs that institutionalize dependency and are building a
stronger world of independent and interdependent human
beings.

CHAPTER 4

Psychology of Money: Where It All Begins

The pursuit and amassing of this . . . (money) is probably the strongest motive-force in our culture. . . . It remains . . . the last of our shameful secrets. Perhaps because of this, the subject, in its personal ramifications, has been very little explored. We have more information about people's intimate sexual behavior than about their money-motivated behavior.

—THOMAS WISEMAN
The Money Motive[1]

WHEN YOU THINK ABOUT MONEY, how do you feel?

Your answer to this seemingly frivolous question is one of the most important factors determining your financial future —for the emotions surrounding money hold a great deal more power over our lives than most of us realize.

The power of money follows us from cradle to grave. We spend a lifetime working for money but rarely understand how and why we use it as we do.

Yet the institutions that control the country's biggest money pools—and to which most of us entrust our money—fully understand the feelings surrounding money and use these feelings.

That's why understanding the emotions of money is as important as understanding the mathematics of money if we are to control our economic destinies.

How you feel about money, in fact, influences how you feel about all of your life. It shapes the way you feel about yourself, your loved ones, your occupation, all the other sources of your income, and your choice of money tools. These feelings shape how you will react to predictable or crisis changes that will occur throughout your lifetime—such changes as marriage, childbirth, divorce, widowhood, and retirement.

And the money emotions that subtly dominate your parents, your spouse, your children, your boss, and the other individuals you deal with daily, shape and distort the discussions and decisions you share with them.

Family counselors say money is one of the greatest sources of family discord. Psychiatrists and psychologists say economic pressures are at the root of much mental illness, and even suicide. In an era when television, magazines, and even dinner party conversations deal openly with homosexuality, adultery, impotence, frigidity, and rape, we still can't deal with our hidden feelings about money. *Money has replaced sex as the source of our most powerful hangups.*

Like sex, money means many different things to each of us—and each of its meanings is charged with such awesome emotions as greed, fear, envy, and guilt.

We desire money as a means to material comfort, power, freedom, prestige—even love and beauty. Or perhaps we desire it simply for "security"—though how much money is enough to feel secure varies from the need to have $2,000 in our checking account to the need to make it through next week.

But at the same time we desire money, we fear it. People have money fears—whether or not they actually have money —and this economic terror is a testament to money's power to control our lives. We fear not having money, for to be poor is to be helpless in a society whose values are determined by the marketplace.

"Being poor," as Michael Harrington points out in his landmark book *The Other America*, "is not one aspect of a person's life in this country, it is his life." Poverty, he says, "twists and deforms the spirit," "destroys aspirations," is "impervious to hope." The poor "are held back by their own pessimism," he adds, for "like the Asian peasant, the impoverished American tends to see life as a fate, an endless cycle from which there is no deliverance."[2]

But we fear having money as well. Life and literature tell us of the double-edged nature of wealth—that it does not bring the satisfactions and pleasures it promises, that it can destroy its owners, that it invites treachery and theft.

A friend of mine, the wife of one of the highest-paid executives in America, keeps her private limousine and chauffeur continuously at her side—not for transportation so much as protection. She is terrified that her wealth will invite a kidnapping.

Our guilts about money spring from our religious and mythological heritage. Many of us were brought up to believe that profits and money-making are evil—that we are somehow "greedy" if we act to protect our self-interest or realize a gain on our lifelong investments of time, money, and ability.

Our lives are shaped not only by our own reactions to money but also the ways other people in our lives react to money. Money and marriage have an intimate connection throughout history. Once betrothals were arranged with the parents' profit motives in mind. Today, most people no longer marry for money—but many stay married for money.

After years of house-buying, child-raising, investing, and premium-paying, a man and wife may find that this "union of monies" keeps them glued together more tightly than affection. "Where a couple has just enough money for their life together," Thomas Wiseman says in *The Money Motive*, "a separation, involving the setting up of two establishments in place of one, entails such financial upheaval that many unhappily married people put up with their situation rather than face the alternative. The choice before them is usually between continuing as they are, or separating and both accepting a drastic reduction in their standard of living. In these circumstances, unless there is a more compelling factor, such as one or the other partner falling in love with someone else, the usual decision is to make do. . . . They may even arrive at the sort of mutual accommodation that produces reasonable contentment."[3]

Money is also intimately connected with control—the control we have over others or the control others have over us; next to physical coercion with armaments, it is probably *the* most powerful and subtle weapon available for achieving control over others. He or she who controls our supply of money, who can increase or decrease its amount, or cut us off altogether, is in many ways our master.

The money control our employers have over our lives is brought home to me each time I ask the women in my workshops to have their husbands question the details of their company pension plans. Many husbands respond by saying they are afraid they will lose their jobs if they ask too many questions.

Most of us unconsciously acquire money emotions during our formative years. Every family has "money characters": the spendthrift sister-in-law, the miserly uncle, the rich oldster who uses money reins to exercise control or "buy" affection. I recall one wealthy patriarch who literally ran the lives of his children throughout his lifetime with the carrot stick of his checkbook. At his death these beneficiaries found a will with powerful restrictions that continued his control virtually from the grave. One could almost visualize the ghost of this crusty old man haunting his son's house, demanding an explanation for each financial decision. The daughter-in-law so resented this weapon of extraterrestrial money power that she swore she would never let either her husband or their children touch a penny of their generous bequests.

Every family also experiences some variety of the pain and suffering that the absence of money can bring—be it debt, unemployment, theft, fire, illness, or death. The power of money, in fact, becomes painfully clear when a family has to settle an estate; a contested bequest of a mere thousand dollars, for instance, can ruin a lifetime family relationship.

As we grow up we are bombarded with advice on how to handle our money. Sons are taught that they must assume responsibility—and provide protection—for their families. Daughters are lectured on how to handle household budgets. Our neighbors, friends, and relatives dish out tips on bargains and money schemes. But no one tells us how to recognize and cope with the emotions that lie under the surface of our financial lives. No one tells us where to go with a money problem.

(Simply because of this dearth of psychological and financial therapy for money problems, I have recommended that employers establish in-house financial counseling services—just as many have initiated alcoholism counseling services. These financial counselors would be experts without an ax to grind whom workers could consult on specific problems such as debts, but on whom they could also rely for help in lifetime economic planning and in such crises as illnesses and deaths in their families.)

The secrecy surrounding money means that the subject of money remains under wraps in many families. As a consequence, some husbands crack or run away under money pressures. Most of them bear the burdens of breadwinning silently—partly because they were brought up to believe that it was part of "man's role" as proud provider, and often partly from the shame of admitting that they too are confused by the complexities of money. Wives are often afraid to ask questions about family finances, for fear of seeming distrustful. Yet wives and children often haven't an inkling of their family's financial worth—even though they're expected to "live within our income."

Daily I see money anxieties, fears, frustrations—and an overwhelming sense of futility—on the pained faces of the women who attend my workshops.

One middle-aged woman felt her husband was going to

divorce her for a younger woman. She didn't understand anything about family finance and was frightened that she would
emerge from divorce with nothing.

"I don't want to hurt my husband," she told me, "for I still
love him. But I've got to protect myself and find out about
our money. I feel so guilty, because as soon as he leaves home
I go through his drawers and the desk to see if I can find any
records that would give me a clue as to what we own."

She added that whenever she sought advice from personal
contacts, she couldn't get answers. Her confusion and frustra-
tion and the pressure of time running out on her marriage
came together in her plaintive cry: "I feel like I'm in a small
room with the walls closing in."

A woman who has spent her life as a dependent is panicked
by the ever-present possibility that her provider may lose his
job, or have an accident, divorce her, or die. The challenge of
controlling her economic life immobilizes her with fear—for
she knows the "money game" is something she has no knowledge or experience to deal with.

Some women react to this terror by dismissing the subject.
"Money is evil," they tell themselves, or "Money isn't really
important." Underneath these rationalizations is the realistic
fear of playing the money game when they don't know the
rules and haven't had any practice.

Yet when they have overcome their fears and set out to
learn the rules, many women find themselves stifled and
frustrated. When they ask the "experts" for help, they are
often belittled and shunted aside as "neurotic females." Ele-
mentary questions about the mechanics of money elicit only a
patronizing smile and a pat on the hand: "Don't you worry
your pretty little head about this, dear. We'll take care of it
for you," they're told.

That was exactly the answer another woman received when
she sought advice on preparing for her ill and dying husband's
eventual death. She explained her problem: "My husband was
a self-employed professional man who could make all the

decisions in corporate finance but never knew anything about our family finances. We have a sizable estate, and I'm just trying to do the homework for him because he's too sick, and I want to know how to handle things when he's gone. I know I should be doing things now, but everywhere I go everyone says, 'Don't bother your pretty head about this.' "

But women aren't the only ones who are given patronizing, "non-think" answers to their money queries. More than most of us realize, our money emotions have become marketing tools used to control us.

We are controlled by the exploitation of our money emotions—our fears, guilt, greed—and our ignorance about the mechanics of money.

Business plays on our emotions in two ways—in our roles as consumers and in our roles as employees.

Where our money lives are concerned with consumption, the head often loses the battle to the heart, simply because of the power money emotions have in our lives. Grocery stores use attractive displays to capitalize on our impulse buying. Cosmetic and apparel manufacturers appeal to our desire for beauty rather than the logic of durable wear.

Where our money lives are concerned as employees—or, in a larger sense, as citizens of our government—we are prey to the psychological fear that we are incapable of handling our own economic lives. We are thus easily convinced that we can't do it for ourselves, that we are incapable of setting aside for our futures. So swayed by money emotions, we let our money be transformed from "our" money into "their" money.

How often have we surrendered authority over our economic lives in response to the appeal of "getting something for nothing," or the comfortable assurance that "we'll take care of it for you"? How often have we acquiesced in making a purchase because we were made to feel guilty about our "economic obligations"?

The sales manual of one of the nation's largest insurance

companies trains agents to use emotion rather than logic to close sales. "What sets him [the prospect] up . . . is the 'gut shot,' the left hook to the solar plexus . . . hitting him in the heart, appealing to his emotions rather than just logic alone," the manual advises.

The words of a sample "sincere emotional appeal" follow, ending with the agent quoting the price of the monthly premium. The agent is then advised to shut up, to let the appeal to the heart sink in. He is told to look down at the selling material for five minutes and let the prospect fight out the emotional battle inside: "Let the inner pressure work on him, the Ego and the Id fight, Id saying, 'I want to join the golf club,' the Ego saying, 'But golly, the kids' education is so important,' the Id saying, 'Yeah, but Dad needs to live a little bit too,' and the Ego, the good guy, always coming back and saying, 'Listen, bad guy. That's selfish. Which is more important?' "

On the other hand, this sales manual cautions an unsuccessful sales pitch is one that gives the prospect too many facts. That technique "causes confusion and a confused mind won't buy."

The training manual further suggests that an agent is not being "professional" if he explains too much to his sales prospects.

Withholding information is the key to sales, the agent learns. He is even given a formula that has become the unwritten password throughout the insurance industry: *K.I.S.S. —Keep It Simple, Stupid.* The formula carries a double entendre: You're stupid, Mr. Agent, if you don't keep it simple, because your prospects are stupid.

Keeping the appeal simple and emotional and treating you as stupid is the way most of the nation's big benefit pools stay in business. Whether the subject is pension plans or Social Security, insurance or annuities, the appeal is emotional—for "protection" or "safety" or "riches" or a "carefree retirement sitting in the sunset."

But this may change as more and more women begin to question the money motives that affect our personal lives and that are used against us as sales gimmicks. Meanwhile, women's questions about the money mathematics that control our lives are stripping away the shrouds of secrecy surrounding the money facts.

To admit one's ignorance is the beginning of wisdom. A woman can admit she knows nothing about money without shame—for, according to the popular stereotype, she was never supposed to know anything about money anyway.

In contrast, up to now a man could not admit he was often confused about money. Realistically, of course, he could hardly be expected to fathom all the complex economic factors that shape our lives—when even the experts flounder outside their own areas of expertise. Nevertheless, popular mythology cast a man as a failure if he didn't know all the answers a provider should know. He certainly couldn't admit, or discuss, his confusion with his wife and family.

Women's search for economic answers is paving the way for more open family communication about money. By asking questions, women are making question-asking legitimate for both sexes. By admitting their ignorance, women are showing others that they are not alone in their own confusion.

Women are taking the subject of money from under the table and putting it on top of the table. They are probing our money emotions and throwing light on the money facts. With an understanding of our money motives, we and our families can feel positively rather than negatively about our economic lives. And, what's more, we can learn to use our money attitudes to help us rather than hurt or hinder us.

PART II

By Choice Or Chance: Your Money Sources

••••➤➡◉⬅◀••••

CHAPTER 5

Time Is Money

Time is the most valuable thing a man can spend.

—THEOPHRASTUS, 278 B.C.

Remember that time is money.

—BEN FRANKLIN, 1748

THE ONE THING that each of us will have equally today is *time—all human beings have equal rights in time.*

We each will have sixty minutes in each hour and twenty-four hours in each day. No one will receive more time and no one will receive less time in this day. The difference is in how we use our time—and how many days we will have to use.

Time is the most powerful and valuable money tool you will have throughout your life. It is probably the one money tool you never thought about or even considered as a money tool. The power of time and the high cost of overlooking its significance are little understood in lifetime financial planning.

Strange we should understand it so little, because the sages and philosophers through the ages have left us words of wisdom relative to time. In fact, *Bartlett's Familiar Quotations* has six columns, over 450 quotations, on time.

To effectively plan your economic future you will need to understand the use of this money tool—*time.*

Time and money are the foundation of the major financial pools: insurance, investments, banks, savings and loans, and pension funds.

The key factors in the profits of most businesses include:

- Volume (selling to many people)
- Markup (selling at a high profit)
- Time (use of money over a long period)

Some businesses are based on one of these marketing premises—but obviously if a business can be built on two or perhaps all three, the more profitable a business will be.

Time should be at the foundation of your economic life also; it is vital to understanding the mathematics of your insurance plans, pension funds, Social Security deposit, and retirement plans.

It is the key to determining your human life value.

You don't have to be an Einstein to understand this economic concept of time. The following chart will help make clear the impact and mathematics of time and money. To help you understand the high cost of overlooking or losing time, look at the Ten-Year Goal Plan chart below. It shows what you can accumulate by putting a value on yourself of only 52¢ an hour.

If you put aside 52¢ an hour for
8 hours a day
7 days a week,
you will be accumulating
$125 a month
$1,500 a year
And if you put this money to work
at 7½ percent compounded continuously
(that is at 7.9 percent effective
annual yield)
for only 10 years,
you will accumulate the following sums:

TEN-YEAR GOAL PLAN[1]

Deposit from Ages	By Age 65 You Will Have Accumulated
0–10	$1,528,290
10–20	714,482
20–30	334,023
30–40	156,157
40–50	73,004
50–60	34,129
60–65 (5 years only)	9,476

This Time and Money Plan is fascinating as well as startling. It tells us many things.

Using this as a basis of Human Life Value you can see that if you began to value your time at age 20—for only ten years—you would have $334,023 at age 65! If you waited until age 30 to establish your Human Life Value you could accumulate $156,157—a substantial amount, but you can clearly see that you would lose $177,866 by losing ten years' time.

If you want to determine how much you would have if you deposited this amount annually *until* age 65, you would add the balance of the years—for example, if you started at age 20 and continued depositing until age 65 (as you would do under Social Security—the maximum deposit today being over $1,700 annually) you would have $706,789.

If you started at age 40 and continued until 65, you would have $116,609; starting at age 50 to 65 you would have $43,605.

Parents or grandparents planning a child's future could start at birth; $1,528,290 could be accumulated at 65 after only ten years (0–10) of deposits.

These figures are based on 7½ percent interest, an amount guaranteed by most banks and savings and loans today.

You can see the power of money over time even more vividly by comparing the difference only one year makes. The foregoing chart assumed that the $1,500 annual deposit was

made at the *beginning* of the year. But if these deposits were
made at the *end* of the year, the accumulation over time
would be significantly smaller.

TEN-YEAR GOAL PLAN

	By Age 65 You Will
Deposit from Ages	Have Accumulated
0–10	$1,416,367
10–20	662,157
20–30	309,561
30–40	144,721
40–50	67,658
50–60	31,630

. Thus the one-year difference between depositing at the
beginning and depositing at the end of each year will net a
gain or loss of $24,462 at age 65 if you accumulate between
ages *20 and 30.*

To use your money tool of *time* most effectively you should
also be aware of the difference a seemingly small change in
interest rates can make in your total accumulation. Too many
of us leave our money in low interest-paying vehicles—we
shrug our shoulders as if to say, "What difference can 1 percent really make?" A big difference, that's what.

Again, to use our Ten-Year Time and Money Goal Plan, if
you deposited this at 6¼ percent instead of the 7½ percent
figure used before, you would see the following accumulations:

TEN-YEAR GOAL PLAN

	By Age 65 You Will
Deposit from Ages	Have Accumulated
0–10	$631,203
10–20	339,495
20–30	182,599
30–40	98,211
40–50	52,823
50–60	28,411
60–65	8,815

Shockingly less, for the same time (10 years), same amount of money (52¢ per hour), but different interest rate.

If you would like to figure what you could accumulate at another rate, use the Rule of 72—a rule of thumb to determine approximately how long it takes your money to *double*. Just divide the percentage into 72. For example:

> 4% divided into 72 = 18 years to double
> 5% divided into 72 = 14 years to double
> 6% divided into 72 = 12 years to double
> 8% divided into 72 = 9 years to double
> 12% divided into 72 = 6 years to double

As an example: if you are 45 years old and you have $10,000 earning 4 percent, you will have accumulated approximately $20,000 at age 63 (eighteen years to double). If you have that same money earning 7½ percent (also guaranteed amount), you will have accumulated over $40,000 by age 65.

Same money, different interest. Increase in asset: $20,000.

All the foregoing charts are computed without taking taxes into account. As you will see in later chapters, you can devise tools to save or defer taxes on your accumulated Human Life Value—through, for instance, the Individual Retirement Account discussed in Business Economics.

One other thought on time and money: whatever money tool you use, I encourage you to use a system that is automatic and systematic such as automatic transfer from checking account, payroll deduction, or other automatic device.

This is the system that Social Security, pension funds, insurance companies, and the IRS use—all are removed weekly from your check. When the insurance industry started using direct bank transfers for private insurance plans, their policy lapses dropped markedly.

Get yourself on automatic because new patterns and disciplines (in other words, good habits) are difficult to start and maintain. Habits rule our lives, as anyone who has ever tried to quit smoking or give up desserts can attest. You have to get yourself "hooked" on the good habit of accumulating for yourself.

The task may seem overwhelming, when you look at the monthly and yearly sums involved, but it's possible if you set your mind to it. I remember one man and wife who were determined to get out of the habit of spending beyond their means. They put themselves on a cash-only basis—and at the end of every day put their excess cash in a kitty which went into a savings account. After only a few years, they had not only drastically reduced their volume of monthly bills and dunning letters but had saved $30,000!

The task also takes a healthy dose of great expectations. Most of us never imagine we could accumulate sums of $30,000 to $300,000 or more over our lifetimes because we are accustomed to thinking of ourselves as staying forever on a subsistence-level merry-go-round.

Yet in a society that encourages and trains us carefully in *progressive debt*, it is important to train *yourself* in *progressive accumulation*.

CHAPTER 6

Money at the Root:
Your Money Sources

In its simplest terms, economics is the study of how man earns
his daily bread.

—ROBERT L. HEILBRONER
The Economic Problem[1]

OUR PERSONAL ECONOMIC SYSTEM is so complex that it is almost
impossible for anyone, man or woman, to understand the
many facets of today's economic life. In our age of financial
specialization, even the experts I interviewed knew little beyond their area of expertise.

We've come a long way from barter—through wampum,
tobacco, various forms of metals, coins, and currency; to
credit, paper checks, plastic cards, the transfer payment
system; and finally toward a cashless society and income
maintenance. (Today 45 percent of the $394.2 billion federal
budget goes to income security for individuals.)

Business and government are continuously finding new
ways for us to become more effective "money machines." In
the process, our personal economic lives are becoming danger-
ously complex and beyond our control.

We know we are earning more income than we ever thought
possible—but we also know we have less. We budget, we
save, we work diligently. We consume books and articles on
money management. The money books tell us how to budget,
pick the right stocks, choose an insurance policy, and spend
our money.

Everyone has become *the* authority on money—your neighbor, your co-worker, your hairdresser, and the cab driver. The movement of the stock market and the economy are the "in" conversations at dinner parties.

What we don't know, deep down, is where our paycheck and checkbook fit into this economy—how we as individuals count. We are taunted by the feeling that something is missing from our financial education, because we know we should be, but are not, making it. We feel trapped and helpless.

Where can we find the necessary information? How do we begin to put the pieces together? Who can we go to for advice?

The wealthy have their professional financial advisors— sometimes with different interests, viewpoints, and answers. The poor have the family service associations, credit counselors, and various community agencies, but such aids are usually sought when it is too late or nearly so—in a debt-counseling or survival situation. The average person has nowhere to go and finds it difficult to receive any kind of professional advice because of limited assets or resources. Even if one has access to top financial advisors one would find that

• No one knows *all* the answers.
• There are no instant answers to financial problems.
• No two people are alike; there are varying degrees of economic status and problems (and they can change quickly); different educational and occupational levels; different lifestyles and cultures, as well as widely different factors involved.

Our money lives are in fact so much more complex than they were even a generation or two ago, that our great-grandparents, were they to return to life today, would be hopelessly confounded by the many new terms, tools, and technology that have been added to our economic lives.

There are, however, basic guidelines that each person can use to design a plan to direct and control his or her own life.

It involves a different way of analyzing and using assets and liabilities. It is not money management—budgeting, saving, spending. Economic life planning requires a new way of thinking about and valuing one's economic and financial life.

I call it analyzing one's *Human Life Value.*

It means analyzing the cost/value of your life as a corporation would analyze the cost/value of its business. What *deposits* are you making and what *benefits* are you receiving in return? And how can you maximize your benefits?

The first step is to separate and analyze those *money sources* that will affect your economic life.

(I searched for eight years for a simple way to analyze and organize the understanding of our money sources. Imagine my surprise when I suddenly found a few months ago that the essential simplicity was discovered centuries ago by Aristotle! He broke down *money sources* into kingdom, government, state, and private citizens[2]—as I have divided the sources into personal, business, and government, seen below. It only proves the old maxim that there's nothing new under the sun!)

Throughout your economic life all money flows to you and from you through three separate *money sources.* (The standard asset/liability personal financial statement form is so structured as to commingle our three separate *money sources* and thus obscure their distinctions.) You must learn to separate the three, as each plays a vital role in your economic future and has an entirely different impact on your life. They are as follows[3]:

Personal Economics

These are assets and liabilities accumulated through your personal financial decisions. These funds usually pass to you and from you through ownership, will, deed, and contract. Your *personal economic money sources* are *affected or con-*

trolled by your access to income, ownership, contract, property, and inheritance. They include the following:

banking, investments, insurance, real estate, credit, loans, trusts.

Business Economics

These are assets and liabilities accumulated through your employee contributions and your employer's contributions or business agreement.

These funds usually pass to and from you by contract, fringe benefits, or business agreements.

Your *business economic money sources* are *affected or controlled* by occupation, wages, and fringe benefits. They include the following:

salaries; commissions; sick leave; pensions; buy and sell agreements; royalties; and group life, health, and disability insurance.

Government Economics

These assets and liabilities usually pass to and from you by law.

Your *government economic money sources* are *affected or controlled* by currency, taxation, and such insurance vehicles as Medicare, Welfare, and Social Security, and a maze of regulations, limitations, qualifications, and laws. They include the following:

Social Security, veterans' benefits, federal and state income tax, property tax, sales tax, state inheritance tax, federal estate tax.

Check off your *money sources* on the following checklists. This will help you organize and analyze your three separate *money sources*.

PERSONAL ECONOMICS
BANKS • SAVINGS AND LOANS • CREDIT UNIONS

Document	*Additional Information*
SAVINGS ACCOUNTS	
_____Statement Accounts	Ownership (in whose name(s))
_____Passbook Accounts	Interest Rate
_____Time Certificates	Time of Certificate
_____Location of Passbooks	Note Type of Account: Regular, Automatic Savings, Retirement, Christmas Club, etc.
CHECKING ACCOUNTS	
_____Location of Bank Statements	Ownership (in whose name(s))
_____Location of Checkbooks	Purpose of Account
_____Government Bonds	As above Date of Maturity
LOANS	
_____Installment	Note: Collateral
_____Auto	Is there Credit Life Insurance
_____Mortgage	on any loans
_____Check Overdraw	
_____Bank Cash Advance	
_____Student Loan	
_____Other	
PERSONAL LOANS AND NOTES OTHERS OWE YOU	
_____Notes and Receipts	Borrower Note: Collateral
YOU OWE OTHERS	
_____Notes and Receipts	Lender Note: Collateral
CREDIT CARDS	
_____Master Charge	Note: Credit Card indebtedness
_____BankAmericard	
_____Department Stores	

PERSONAL ECONOMICS
BANKS • SAVINGS AND LOANS • CREDIT UNIONS

Document	Additional Information
——Oil Companies	
——American Express	
——Carte Blanche	
——Diners Club	
——Other	
——Travelers Checks	
——Certified Checks	
——Cashiers Checks	

SAFE DEPOSIT BOX

——Safe Deposit Key	In whose name(s)
——Box Inventory	Person with access or power of
——Safe Deposit Number	attorney

TRUSTS CREATED BY YOU
FOR OTHERS

——Records located at:	Revocable or irrevocable.
	Purpose and nature of property.
	Beneficiary, Trustee, Attorney

CREATED BY OTHERS
FOR YOU

——Records located at:	As above

TRUSTS OF WHICH SPOUSE
IS TRUSTEE

——Records located at:	As above

INSURANCE AND INVESTMENTS

Document	Additional Information
INSURANCE—LIFE	
——Ownership by me on my life	Note: Beneficiary,
——Ownership by others on my life	Amount, Loans on Policy, Assigned as Security, Type of
——Owned by me on others	Policy, Term or
——Payable to estate	Permanent

_____National Service Life
　　　(G.I.)
_____Accidental Death
_____Association or Fraternal
_____Equity Linked Policy
_____Variable Annuities
_____Student Loan Insurance

INSURANCE—HEALTH
_____Basic Hospital　　　　　　Note: Limits of Benefits
_____Major Medical
_____Hospital Indemnity
_____Surgical Insurance
_____Accident Insurance
_____Disability Insurance
_____Student Health Insurance
_____Association or Fraternal
　　　Medical Benefits
_____Other

INSURANCE—CASUALTY
_____Homeowners　　　　　　Note: Limits of Benefits
_____Auto
_____Business Property
_____Other

INVESTMENTS
_____Common Stock　　　　　Ownership (in whose name(s))
_____Preferred Stock　　　　　Number of Shares
_____Corporate Bonds　　　　Current Market Value
_____Privately Held Stock　　　Yearly Income
_____Convertible Bonds　　　　Profit or Loss
_____Municipal Bonds
_____Mutual Funds
_____Other

REAL ESTATE AND PERSONAL PROPERTY

Document　　　　　　　*Additional Information*

REAL ESTATE
_____Residence　　　　　　Location of: Deed,
_____Apartment House　　　Copy of Mortgage, Title
_____Business Building　　　Abstract, Title Insurance

REAL ESTATE AND PERSONAL PROPERTY

Document	*Additional Information*
_____Raw Land _____Other	Policy, Improvement and Maintenance Receipts, Survey, Property Management, Tax Receipts, Leases, Security, Receipts, Rent Deposits

_____OIL LEASES

_____GAS LEASES

_____MINERAL LEASES

PERSONAL PROPERTY
_____Jewelry
_____Valuable Antiques
_____Valuable Art
_____Furniture
_____Property in Storage

AUTOMOBILES
_____Title and Registration

BILLS OF SALE
(Be sure to note any of the
above loaned to others)

BUSINESS ECONOMICS
EMPLOYEE BENEFITS

Document

HISTORY OF EMPLOYMENT	YEARS OF EMPLOYMENT
_____Private Industry	_____
_____Self Employed	_____
_____Federal Government	_____
_____State Government	_____
_____Local Government	_____
_____Railroad	_____
_____Union	_____

INCOME
_____Unpaid Wages
_____Accumulated Paid
    Vacation
_____Sick Leave
_____Bonuses
_____Commissions
_____Royalties
_____Patent Rights

DEFERRED INCOME
_____Deferred Compensation
_____Deferred Bonus
_____Qualified Stock Options
_____Nonqualified Stock
    Options
_____Profit Sharing
_____Other

INSURANCE—LIFE
_____Group Life Insurance
_____Group Accident Insurance
_____Group Travel Insurance
_____Union Life Insurance

INSURANCE—HEALTH
_____Basic Hospital
_____Major Medical
_____Accident Health Insurance
_____Disability Insurance
_____Workmen's Compensation
_____Union Health Insurance

PENSIONS—PRESENT EMPLOYER
_____Monthly Income
_____Vested Benefits
_____Survivor Benefit Option
_____Union Pension

PENSIONS—PAST EMPLOYERS
_____Monthly Income
_____Vested Benefits
_____Survivor Benefit Option
_____Former Union Pensions

BUSINESS ECONOMICS
EMPLOYEE BENEFITS

Document

PERSONAL RETIREMENT
PLANS—QUALIFIED
    (Tax Deductible) paid by
    Employee Contribution
_____TSA (Teachers)
_____IRA H.R. 10
_____Thrift Plan (tax-free
    growth)
_____Other
_____Past Employers

PERSONAL PAYROLL
SAVINGS PLAN
_____Credit Union
_____Bank or Savings and Loan
_____Government Bonds
_____Investment Plans
_____Insurance Plans
_____Annuities

SELF EMPLOYED
_____Buy and Sell Agreement
    (how funded)
_____Agreement for
    Continuation of Business
_____Ownership Distribution
_____Income Agreement
_____Accounts Receivable
_____Equipment or Furniture
_____Business Loans,
    Personally Responsible
    for
_____Husband's Business
    Loans, Wife Responsible
    for

GOVERNMENT ECONOMICS
GOVERNMENT PAPERS

Document

SOCIAL SECURITY
_____Social Security Number
_____Husband
_____Wife
_____Children
_____Dependents
_____Social Security Card
_____Social Security Papers
_____Present Monthly Benefits

VETERANS PAPERS
_____Discharge Papers
_____Service Dates
_____Pension Benefit Records
_____V.A. Claim Number
_____Military Service Number
_____Branch of Service

INCOME TAX RETURNS
_____Federal
_____State
_____Property
_____Worksheet and Evidence
of Support (last 3 years)

ESTATE TAX
_____Location of Papers

INHERITANCE TAX
_____Location of Papers

GIFT TAX
_____Location of Papers

After you have listed and analyzed your money sources, you must understand how these sources can change.

Which of these money sources will begin, which will end, which will continue with crises or life changes?

For instance, in the event of widowhood, your life insurance benefits will begin; your spouse's income will end; your investment and savings growth will continue. Your rent or mortgage payment will continue. Will your spouse's survivor pension or Social Security benefits begin? If he is self-employed, will you receive income from the business, or will you be responsible for the debts of his business?

With each of these money sources, a woman has a varying degree of control and benefits, depending on the laws, factors, money vehicles, contracts, wills, etc., involved.

The following "Twenty-five Steps to Personal Economic Planning" will help you understand your money sources and organize, evaluate, and plan your economic future.

Twenty-five Steps to Personal Economic Planning

ORGANIZE THE FACTS

1. Understand, list and analyze all your money sources
2. Separate each money source by:
    A. *Personal Economics*—savings, investments, insurance, real estate, etc.
    B. *Business Economics*—salary, pensions, profit sharing, group insurance, business agreements, royalties, etc.
    C. *Government Economics*—Social Security, income tax, property tax, etc.
3. Establish a central location for all data, records, and documents

EVALUATE YOUR OBJECTIVES

4. Know how each money source is held (ownership in whose name), percentage of contribution by each spouse

5. Know the status changes of each money source upon crisis changes: widowhood, illness, unemployment, divorce, etc.
6. Understand which of these money sources will end, which will begin, and which will continue
7. Identify problem areas: lack of liquidity, funding for education, retirement planning, etc.
8. Adopt solutions and alternative options

PLAN YOUR ECONOMIC FUTURE

9. Know your spouse's financial advisors: lawyer, accountant, banker, stock broker, insurance broker
10. Determine specific retirement plans
11. Review your insurance needs: life, health, disability, and property insurance; evaluate need for change of ownership, beneficiary designation; understand settlement options, policy loans, etc.
12. Understand what Social Security benefits you are eligible for: inclusions, exclusions, years without coverage
13. Complete and update wills
14. Determine the objectives of your estate plan
15. Know what money sources will be included in each spouse's taxable estate
16. Understand state inheritance tax laws and federal estate tax laws
17. Determine use of trusts
18. Understand and determine lifetime transfers (gifts)
19. Determine who you will select as
    Executor
    Co-Executor
    Trustee
    Guardian of minor children
20. Determine beneficiaries and what assets you wish to distribute to each

21. Write a letter of instruction; a letter of personal wishes to your family
22. Family communication: Are there any difficult family members, family feuds? Have you discussed inheritance or gifts with the other family members involved?

BUSINESS ECONOMIC PLANNING

23. Have a thorough knowledge of employee benefits; understand group life, hospital, and disability insurance; understand pension plans, profit sharing, in regard to vesting requirements, benefit formulas, and how changes can effect same
24. If spouse is self-employed, understand existing business agreements for continuation of business, buy and sell agreements
25. Know what business debts you or estate will be responsible for

CHAPTER 7

The Money Stages in Your Life

Qualities which the head of a household must possess with his property; Firstly, he must have the faculty of *acquiring* and, secondly, that of *preserving* what he has acquired; otherwise, there is no more benefit in acquiring than in bailing with a colander, or in the proverbial wine jar with a hole in the bottom. Thirdly and fourthly, he must know how to improve his property and how to make use of it since these are the ends for which the powers of acquisition and preservation are sought.

—ARISTOTLE
oikonomia[1]

FEW OF US THINK of our life stages in terms of money. For most of us the *money stages* of our lives have meant stepping up to progressively higher levels of consumption, taxation, and payments to group business and insurance pools. During our lifetime, whether our family income is $200 a month or $20,000 a year, outside factors and requirements often beyond our control seem to leave us with little or nothing to accumulate for ourselves.

Regardless of our incomes, we have become so used to living just barely within our means, at "subsistence levels," that we are almost preconditioned to believe that we *cannot* accumulate anything for ourselves. Consequently, we often live with the gnawing fear of "what if something should happen?"

In his *Economics*, Campbell R. McConnell attests to the reality of these fears, in the section "The Unequal Distribution of Misfortune": "A host of economic hazards in such forms as prolonged illness, serious accident, death of the family breadwinner, and unemployment may plunge a family into relative poverty."[2]

I found this subsistence-level living and unfocused fear as prevalent in the Bel Air circuit as I did in the modest families of East Los Angeles. Sometimes the fear was even greater in the Bel Air circuit, where keeping up with the neighbors required a highly mortgaged home, heavily dependent on a consistent high income, as well as a concomitant life-style consisting of the most expensive schools, a country club membership, elegantly appointed interiors, and, of course, at least two cars. Many of these families were in hock up to their ears. Their progressive debt-conditioning had made progressive accumulation impossible.

Throughout your life you will go through four different but closely interwoven *money stages*:

1. Accumulation
2. Growth
3. Income
4. Conservation/Distribution

At many points of your life you may be going through several stages simultaneously.

Accumulation is the stage all of us begin with, and most of us continue struggling with for the rest of our lives.

("When I was making $125 a week," a young reporter told me recently, "I thought my wife and I could live like millionaires on $300 a week. But now that we earn that, we still aren't making it.")

Obviously, without this stage none of the others are possible. That is why setting a Human Life Value on ourselves as early as possible is a key factor in our accumulation stage (as you could clearly see from the Time and Money Ten-Year Goal Plan). Again I urge you to set up the instrument of accumulation on a systematic and automatic basis for purposes of discipline, habit, continuity, and goal completion.

Growth is the obvious next step in the process, but not so obvious is which money tool you should select for growth.

Psychological as well as financial factors are equally important in this decision. Do you want this money in a risk position, with the hope (but no guarantee) of bringing a high return? Or would you feel better with this money in a safety position?

If you choose a safety instrument, you should select the instrument that brings you the highest guaranteed interest because, remember, it will take 14 years for your 5 percent money to double and 9.1 years for your $7\frac{1}{2}$ percent money to double.

The difficulty in accumulating money to a growth position today was reflected in a plaintive tale a young advertising executive told me. His growth objective was a home for his family (instead of renting an apartment). "When my father was my age, he made much less than I am earning now," he said, "but he bought a house—which has appreciated considerably—a membership in the country club, and has always had a good life. My wife and I have been saving for five years to buy a house, and yet the market value of homes is going up so much faster than our savings are growing that we still can't afford a down payment."

Income is the stage at which you will need to withdraw money for living and everyday expenses. Generally, this will happen with retirement. It could, of course, happen with widowhood, or other life changes when you would have to draw income from your property. The need for income is sometimes the first time a woman becomes aware of the importance of liquidity. Is there enough cash immediately available to meet expenses or would you have to liquidate an asset for income? Which asset would you be best advised to liquidate? Should you sell your house? Should you sell your stocks at a loss, or sacrifice your potential future profit in a rising market? Should you keep or sell your spouse's busi-

ness? There are varying factors that could affect your financial
decisions during the income stage.

Conservation/Distribution is arranging for the transfer of
your assets to your family and loved ones in accordance
with your wishes and with the least possible cost during your
lifetime or upon your death. This is the area that women
seem to know least about. We often assume that this stage
is only for the old, the married, or the rich. I have seen
families work for a lifetime to acquire their wealth and lose a
sizable amount of their property due to ignorance of money
mechanics.

A shocking case was brought to my attention at one of my
bank workshops. An elderly woman told me of her widower
brother who had been a farmer all his life. The farm had
grown to a sizable market value and upon his death he left it
to his two daughters—who were forced to sell it to pay the
inheritance taxes. It was the sad old cycle of rags-to-riches-
to-rags in one generation. The old gentleman had invested
the toil, time, and sweat of his life in his farm, but because
he did not know how to conserve this precious investment
and distribute it to his heirs, all was for naught. His very
labors to increase his property's value backfired on him when
the tax assessors considered the increased market value and
established very high estate taxes.

The conservation and distribution of property is equally
important to you if you are a single person or family member
of average means, whether you are planning for the property
you will pass on or helping your family and friends with
property they might pass on to you. And though you may
not think you have anything "valuable" to pass on, remember
there are still sentimental possessions—a piece of family
jewelry or a four-poster bed that would be treasured by one
of your heirs but might be meaningless to others.

PART III

The Systems: Our Protectors
Business Economics

·••——————◉————··•

CHAPTER 8

Take It or Leave It:
The Paycheck

> The labor now performed by the men could not be performed by the women without generations of effort and adaptation. . . . This is not owing to lack of the essential human faculties necessary to such achievements, nor to any inherent disability of the sex, but to the present condition of women, forbidding the development of this degree of economic ability. The male human being is thousands of years in advance of the female in economic status.
>
> —CHARLOTTE PERKINS GILMAN
> *Women and Economics*[1]

THE PAYCHECK IS one of women's and society's most important economic sources. Individuals' economic lives are greatly defined by their jobs.

The paycheck is also one of the most serious areas of economic waste in America.

Today no one is oblivious to the history of women's struggle for equal pay and equal opportunity; but even with public and corporate awareness, backed up by federal laws, women's incomes in ratio to men's are not increasing. They are decreasing, as the following chart shows.

MEDIAN EARNINGS OF WOMEN AND MEN AS FULL-TIME,
YEAR-ROUND WORKERS

Year	Men's Pay	Women's Pay	Women's Pay as Percentage of Men's Pay
1956	$ 4,462	$2,828	63%
1964	6,283	3,710	59%
1974	12,152	6,957	57%

U.S. Department of Commerce.

The causes of low wages, which began when women entered the industrial society, are not that different today. These causes were described by Mary Elizabeth Pidgeon in *Women in the Economy of the U.S.* in 1937 (Department of Labor—Women's Bureau)[2]:

• She was used as fill-in labor—her work patterns were highly seasonal.
• She was traditionally considered of low money value.
• Enterprising entrepreneurs were quick to see their own advantage in employing cheap labor, for the work of women had not received a wage in the home.
• Women did not take jobs away from men; their jobs were concentrated in occupations that were undesirable to men (primarily related to household arts and service).
• When women were paid low wages by an industry, it set a standard of low wages throughout the industry (as in the mills), affecting all the workers.

These causes were the same in 1937 and they are the same now almost 40 years later; *why*?

While for years women struggled for equal wages and work opportunity, few gave thought to the money being withdrawn from their paychecks.

But this too is changing—today's woman is closely examining the cost/value of her deposit and that of her spouse. She is examining past, present, and future benefits.

It is now evident that you cannot begin lifetime economic planning without analyzing what deposits are being taken from your paycheck or what benefits you will be receiving in return; how your wage base, occupation, type of employer, years of service, mobility (changing jobs), and years outside the paid labor force all affect your economic future.

In today's labor market, women have three major economic roles[8]:

1. Contributor (working single women)
2. Contributor/spouse (working wife)
3. Spouse (homemaker, nonpaid labor-force wife).

A woman may, at varying times of her life, participate in all three roles—in which case she should be receiving benefits from all three sources.

In other words, benefits have to be examined from three different viewpoints and lifetime changes.

As a single woman, what benefits will she (herself) receive, and will she be able to pass on benefits to family or heirs?

As a working wife, what benefits will she receive, and what benefits will her spouse and family receive in the event of her death? What benefits will she receive from her husband's work years in the event of widowhood?

As a spouse homemaker, what benefits would she receive as a widow?

It is important to look at the mathematics of today's paycheck to evaluate her cost/value. The following tables show employees' take-home pay and employers' payroll costs, with blanks for you to fill in your own paycheck deposits.

EMPLOYEE'S TAKE-HOME PAY
Wage Rate of $5.00 Per Hour*

		Amount Withheld at Your Wage Rate	
Item	Amount Withheld	Per Hour	Per Pay Period
Federal Income Tax	$0.70		
Social Security	0.29		
State Income Tax*	0.10		
Medical Plan*	0.09		
State Disability Insurance*	0.05		
Life Insurance*	0.02		
Long Term Disability*	0.02		
Supplementary Accident and Disability	0.01		
Total Deductions Per Hour	1.28		
Take-Home Pay Per Hour	3.72		

* Typical situation. Amounts withheld vary from company to company and state to state.

You can clearly see that 40 to 50 percent of your paycheck is being removed before you ever receive a penny. This deduction has two purposes:

1. To establish the present and future economic security of yourself and your family through:

> Pensions
> Social Security
> Life insurance
> Health insurance
> State and/or group disability insurance
> Unemployment insurance
> Vacations, holidays, sick leave

2. To fulfill your responsibility to society through your federal income tax.

The money that the American woman and her family are

depositing toward their present and future economic security
—to insurance companies, pension funds, and government
revenues—represents a major deposit into the economy.

EMPLOYER PAYROLL COST

Wage Rate of $5.00 Per Hour*

Item	Amount Withheld	Amount at Your Wage Rate	
		Hourly	Pay Period
Pension Plan	$0.30	_____	_____
Social Security	0.29	_____	_____
Two-Week Vacation	0.20	_____	_____
Nine Paid Holidays	0.19	_____	_____
Medical Plan	0.18	_____	_____
Sick Leave	0.10	_____	_____
Workmen's Compensation and Unemployment Insurance	0.10	_____	_____
Life Insurance	0.04	_____	_____
Long Term Disability	0.02	_____	_____
Total	1.42	_____	_____
Actual Hourly Pay	6.42	_____	_____
Actual Take-Home Pay	3.72	_____	_____

* Typical situation. Amounts shown above vary from company to
company and state to state.

*When you measure the money that circulates throughout
this country through these three sources, it is a staggering
amount.*

Women are finding that while their deposits into these
sources are enormous, their benefits are pitiful.

To establish your cost/value we will analyze the mathematics of each instrument separately.

In the following chapters we shall examine women's cost/
value from their paycheck deposits into pensions, Social
Security, and fringe benefits.

CHAPTER 9

"Their Money":
The Private Pension System

My earning days are over,
I'm slowly going broke!
What should have been my pension
Was just a puff of smoke.

—MURIEL F. SWIFT
Secretary, forty years in the labor force[1]

THE CONGRESSIONAL RESEARCH SERVICE tells us of the historical development of the private pension system:

"During the first century of American political life—from the beginning of the Revolution to 1875—the economic needs of older citizens were satisfied chiefly by family resources.

"The early attitude of employers toward pension plans was that pensions were gifts to their workers in recognition of 'long and faithful service' and that no legal rights were thereby given to employees who became beneficiaries of a plan."

It continues that "before the 1942 Revenue Act . . . some plans . . . were for the benefit of a few key individuals within companies, which in operation became tax avoidance devices rather than bona fide retirement plans."[2]

The laws have changed, become more rigid, more complex, but for women the actual benefits received still reflect the old *attitudes* that "pensions were gifts with no legal rights" and that they were used as "tax avoidance for the few key individuals."

The pension industry today has become one of our major industries—a $180 billion industry, expected to reach $300 billion by 1980.

With such assets, why are women as widows and workers receiving so little? Why are six out of ten widows living in poverty, with only 2 percent receiving benefits from spouses' working years?

Why is the average pension received by today's woman retiree less than $81 a month—$970 per year?

Why do only 9 percent of today's working women have vested benefits[3]—and at a much lower benefit potential because of their low wage base?

To understand how a $180 billion industry has left women with this below-poverty level status, we must examine our private pension system from its:

- Historic performance
- Corporate purpose
- Present laws

The pension "promise" that began in 1875 did not cover large numbers of people until World War II. The thirty years that have elapsed since then, however, give us a perspective for judging pensions' performance.

For the past few years, newspapers, magazines, and television have vividly detailed the economic nightmare of the worker who had "hopes" and "promises" of receiving income in the retirement years.

The legal loopholes, executive manipulation, and employee ignorance that created this nightmare are familiar to every American—who sees its ravages in his or her own family and community. Few families have escaped the consequences of this dependence on "their money."

The myriad ways you can lose pension benefits have been repeated to me hundreds of times by my students and clients. Here are some actual cases that might help you better understand the risks involved.

MARTHA (Contributor) is a single woman who was a secretary for various small offices all her life. Because of her changing jobs she had no opportunity to build pension benefits. An illness took all the savings she had accumulated at retirement. How does she get by? She lives in a closet-size room in a bleak hotel with a hotplate in the corner—and merely exists. She still lives in the reflected glory of the "exciting" men she worked for in the entertainment and public relation fields.

ELIZABETH (Spouse) is a 70-year-old widow whose husband worked for over fifty years for a company that is not just well-known but revered. Shortly after his death fifteen years ago, the company advised her that her husband's pension would stop, but they wanted to "do something extra for her." They would "send her an additional small amount for the next few months"—*and then nothing.*

This proud lady still does not let this be known to family and friends, because she feels it would be an insult to her husband's dignity and years of dedicated service as well as a stigma for her children, who are extremely successful professionals.

Elizabeth was lucky. She and her husband had planned and accumulated assets throughout their lives, enabling her to be secure in her retirement years despite being cheated of her husband's pension. She still keeps her proud spirit. She still plans wisely. She still doesn't buy; she selects. She keeps her expenses low, while maintaining her lovely apartment by managing the building she lives in and sharing her apartment with a (rent-paying) relative.

Pension tragedies are not just for the elderly. One family's entire economic security was shattered when JOAN's (contributor/spouse) husband, who had been an executive with a prestigious firm, left for an advancement with another firm. But he found to his dismay that his large pension fund, the trophy of eighteen years in his former management position, would not go with him.

When I asked Joan and her husband why they had not sued his former employer, they said they had discussed the case with an attorney but that the exorbitant legal fees had made a lawsuit prohibitive. The former employer had a regulation loophole and refused her husband any type of settlement.

Joan, who had returned to work to put her children through college, realized that her salary would have to replace the family's lost pension instead of adding to its income.

SUSAN (spouse turned contributor) was shocked when she received a $3,000 pension settlement from the large aerospace firm that had employed her husband for thirty years. He died suddenly at 55 of a heart attack. If Susan's husband had lived just five more years, they would have received $900 a month in retirement income. Susan was forced to train for a new career and enter the labor force. Her earnings, of course, came nowhere close to matching the $900 a month she lost through her husband's premature death. To compound the economic waste, she herself was paying into Social Security from her earnings, but would never be able to benefit from her deposits because she would qualify for only one benefit, hers or her husband's. Due to her age, she would not be able to work for her company long enough to be vested before she reached mandatory retirement age.

Standing in sharp contrast to these accounts, there's the happy ending to the pension story of Bob R. Dorsey. Mr. Dorsey, former chairman of Gulf Oil Corporation, was ousted from Gulf when it was revealed that the corporation had made illegal political and foreign payments totaling $12.3 million during Mr. Dorsey's fourteen-year tenure as chairman.

Though he was in effect fired and disgraced, Mr. Dorsey, according to the *New York Times,* "will get a lump sum payment of $1.6 million in retirement benefits . . . an annual pension of $48,158 . . . $54,000 in accumulated vacation pay."[4]

Because of public awareness and pressure for pension change—and revelations of measured economic fraud and misrepresentation—Congress passed in 1974 the new Pension Reform Law commonly known as ERISA (Employee Retirement Income Security Act). This new law applies to four different categories of employees:

1. Employees covered by a qualified pension or profit-sharing plan.
2. Employees without pension plans—eligible for the Individual Retirement Act (IRA).
3. The self-employed—eligible for the Keogh Plan (H.R. 10).
4. Employees changing employment with vested pension funds—rollover pension funds.

It also imposes more stringent requirements on employers for pension fund reporting and disclosure, fiduciary and funding standards, management, participation, vesting, termination, and widow-widower benefits.

Through the Pension Benefit Guarantee Corporation, ERISA insures benefit payments of most pension plans after July 1, 1974. The act does not restore rights and benefits lost before its enactment.

But before we become mesmerized again with "reform" rules and "protections," let's look behind the semantics to the realities and requirements under the qualified pension plan segment that will still leave women and their families in the same relative positions as before ERISA.

We cannot allow this kind of economic rape and havoc to happen again.

First a note on semantics. The private language of pension legislation is strewn with foreign sounding words. Do you know what "fiduciary" means? Or "vesting"? Or "contributory"? I sometimes suspect that the vocabulary of pensions has been made deliberately confusing to throw us off the track in analyzing our cost/value.

As employees we are semantically wooed into participating in pension plans because we believe we are getting "protection" or "security" or "something for nothing." But let's look at their corporate purpose to examine the mathematics of their growth to a $180 billion industry.

Employers' original motives in providing pension plans were to keep their present employees and attract new ones and to provide retirement income for these employees.

The *Women and Poverty* report from the United States Commission on Civil Rights explains how pensions provide another advantage to employers:

Although there is no requirement that an employer establish a pension plan, considerable incentives, namely tax incentives, are offered by the Government to encourage the establishment of pension plans. The tax incentives permit employers to deduct contributions made to the plan on behalf of covered employees; earnings on the assets of the plan are exempt from taxation, and employees defer income tax on pension benefits until they actually are received. Lost tax revenues from these incentives are estimated at a substantial $4 billion annually. Most private pension plans are non-contributory, that is, employers make all the contributions. Because pension benefits are thought of as deferred wages and because of the annual $4 billion tax savings to employers, it can be argued, however, that *everyone pays for pension benefits—taxpayers, consumers, and the employees themselves* [italics added].[5]

This statement tells us several things:

• Employers are not required to establish pension plans (50 percent do not have them).

• It tells us why only 9 percent of working women have vested funds, with the rest of the 27 percent (total 36 percent covered) losing funds when they change jobs.

• When an unvested employee leaves the company, her pension money (deposited in her name) stays with the employer, growing tax free for the employer's benefit (thereby making mobility—changing jobs—a valuable tool for the employer and a costly tool for the employee).

• When retirees are forced to live on a below-survival income (half the women over 65 currently have total annual incomes of less than $2,000—from all sources), they are forced to become welfare recipients. If American women continue to retire on below-survival income, their ability to contribute to the economy is prohibited and their need to withdraw income from the economy is increased.

David Hapgood describes this employer advantage more bluntly in his *The Screwing of the Average Man*:

The employer says: 'If you will give up all or part of a wage increase, I'll put some money aside in a fund, and I'll pay you a pension . . . when you retire. The *employer gets the hard cash* [italics added] and the employees get the promise that will be broken: all of them give up the raise, but only a few will ever collect the pension.[6]

Thus the worker, in effect, has become the corporation's funding agent for the pension system Through sacrifice of her pay raises she increases the corporate pension funds and creates a corporate tax deduction on these monies set aside but rarely collected. In addition to this, when the widow or worker ends up in poverty or on welfare, everyone pays— the worker, the consumer, and the taxpayer.

How did these funds grow to $180 billion? Remember the "Time is Money" chapter; the three factors on which business is built are volume, markup, and time. You can clearly see that the corporation and the pension industry have all three factors working for them. With a volume of over 25 million covered workers, the markup could be as high as 100 percent for the estimated six out of ten workers who will never receive a benefit. And with the phenomenal power of time, these funds will continue to grow over many years for *their* benefit, not yours, with the kind of geometric progression you saw in "Time is Money."

Now we'll look at the requirements and realities of the qualified pension plan segment of the new Pension Reform Law to see how women will fare in the future.

The Department of Labor has produced a booklet, *Often-Asked Questions about the Employees Retirement Income Security Act of 1974*, which you can obtain from the U.S. Department of Labor, Labor-Management Services Administration, Office of Employee Benefits Security, Washington, D.C. 20216. This booklet explains what the private pension segment of ERISA does and does not do.

Let's first examine what the Act does *not* do.

• The Act does not require employers to offer pension plans—it does require those that do to meet certain minimum standards.

• The Act does not guarantee a pension to every worker—only to workers who have satisfied plan requirements which are consistent with the minimum standards of the law.

• It does not set specific amounts of money to be paid out as pensions, and it does not deal with the adequacy of pension benefits—although it does require that a survivor benefit be at least 50 percent of the retirement benefit.

• The Act does not guarantee benefits to all widows—it does not help widows whose spouses are already deceased or retired before enactment date, or widows whose spouses have refused the survivor option.

• Termination insurance does not cover all pension plans—only defined benefit pension plans (those that provide for a fixed pension benefit) which meet other specified standards, and only those which terminate after July 1, 1974.

• The law does not provide that an employee can automatically transfer pensions if changing jobs.

• With few exceptions, the Act does not restore rights and benefits lost before its enactment.

Now let's examine what the plan does do.

To become eligible for pension benefits the employee must first meet the vesting requirements.

Vesting is the right of a pension plan participant to the

accrued pension monies contributed by an employer or union on his or her behalf. This right is usually conditioned on a stated period of service or attainment of a special age, and frequently both.

How will the new vesting requirements affect your ability to accumulate pension funds? How will you be affected by job changes and age?

VESTING REQUIREMENTS

Often-Asked Questions explains that "a pension plan covered by vesting provisions must provide full and immediate vesting of benefits from employee contributions. Employer contributions, except "class year plans" (profit-sharing, stock bonus, and money purchase plans for which each year's contributions vest separately), must vest at least as fast as provided under one of the following three schedules.

• Full (100 percent) vesting after 10 years of service (with no vesting prior to completion of 10 years of service).

• Graded vesting (5–15 years): 25 percent vesting after 5 years of service, plus 5 percent for each additional year of service up to 10 years (50 percent vesting after 10 years), plus an additional 10 percent for each year thereafter (100 percent vesting after 15 years of service).

• Rule of 45 (based on age and service): 50 percent vesting for an employee with at least 5 years of service when his age and years of service add up to 45, plus 10 percent for each year thereafter.

Under any of the options an employee must be at least 50 percent vested after 10 years of service and 100 percent vested after 15 years of service regardless of age.

Class year plans must provide for 100 percent vesting not later than the end of the fifth plan year following the plan year for which contributions are made.

VESTING REALITIES

The realities of a woman's work life automatically prohibit her from pension eligibility.

Labor Department studies show that women's job mobility is twice that of men's. The median years on current jobs for women is 2.8 and for men is 4.6; the median years on current jobs for women over 45 is 6.6 years and for men is 12.7 years.[7]

Thus it is evident that the mobility and stop-start work patterns of women do not even come close to meeting the vesting requirements.

Whether a woman's interrupted work pattern is by choice as a homemaker or by need, due to child or family responsibilities, the private pension portion of ERISA will leave most women with no actual pensions in their own names.

As you can see, the vesting requirements will be difficult or impossible for many husbands to meet as well. The important question you must ask yourself is: How will your mobility work patterns and those of your spouse fit into the prescribed requirements?

Both men and women are penalized by their mobility work patterns. It intrigues me that mobility makes us second-class citizens, ineligible for many of business's benefits, when mobility was one of the foundations of our country. As Blumenthal notes: "From the early days a prime feature of our national development has been mobility. . . . This more than any other influence served to cement the diverse sections of the country with family bonds."[8] I have often wondered how the experts think this country could have been explored or cultivated without mobility.

Today many Americans, the elderly as well as the young, are finally determining their own mobility status, as a recent *Time* cover story announced in "Americans on the Move."[9]

Pensions' penalties for mobility affect not only women

whose work patterns do not coincide with vesting requirements, but also those individuals who wish to change jobs or change locale for personal reasons. These penalties also victimize the millions of corporate employees whose professions often require mobility in employment—writers, photographers, journalists, artists, salesmen, etc. They stifle the young or middle-aged worker seeking advancement who must change companies to move up the corporate ladder.

Mobility, like dependency, is a label and frame of mind that benefits the "authorities" and "systems" and is used to keep the system at a status quo and the worker under control.

Thus we have a "double standard of mobility."

As you recall in analyzing the advantage to the employer, and the disadvantage to the worker, employee mobility was a key factor in the growth of the pension industry and in increasing the amount of monies growing tax free in the company pension fund (because the employee left his or her unvested pension behind when changing jobs).

If we are to have an economic future which we, not the system, control and direct, we must remove the mobility and dependency stigma from our minds and measurements.

Mobility is only one area in which the reform law leaves women in the same secondary pension position they occupied before reform. The other areas include:

- Age requirements
- Part-time or temporary employment requirements
- Integration of private pension plans with
    Social Security
- Break in service requirements.

AGE REQUIREMENTS

Generally, a pension plan must allow an employee to participate when he or she is age 25 and has completed one year of service. Moreover, defined-benefit and target-benefit pension plans are permitted to exclude an employee who is within five years of the normal retirement age under the plan when he is hired.

Another requirement is the Rule of 45, referred to before, which makes vesting dependent on age and service. (See "Vesting Requirements").

AGE REALITIES

According to the *1975 Handbook on Women Workers* published by the Department of Labor, women between the ages of 20 and 24 have the highest labor force participation of any female age group.[10] Over 71 percent of all women in that age range are in the work force. If an employee is not eligible to build pension credits until age 25, it is obvious that the young not only suffer a major pension handicap but also lose the power of time and interest compounding on their behalf. "Time is Money" shows the enormous sums that can be accumulated starting at age 20. (If you accumulate $125 a month for ten years from age 20 to 30 at 7½ percent interest, this will grow to $334,023 by age 65—tax-free growth on your ten-year $15,000 deposit would be $319,023.)

At the other end of the chronological clock, the pension law discriminates against older women. This is indeed ironic since a federal law, the Age Discrimination in Employment Act, "prohibits employers . . . from discrimination on the basis of age against any person between the ages of 40 and 65 in hiring, firing, promotion, or other aspect of employment."

Nevertheless, the Rule of 45 formula could present many closed doors to the middle-aged woman seeking employment. The employer using that formula might think twice about hiring an employee who would have to receive 50 percent vesting sooner than other, younger employees.

Still further along the age scale, the older woman worker

may never have the opportunity to qualify for pension benefits if her vesting begins after ten or fifteen years of work.

At almost any age, the woman worker will find obstacles that block her from pension fund eligibility.

PART-TIME OR TEMPORARY EMPLOYMENT REQUIREMENTS

Before vesting, an employee can be required to put in a year of service, defined as a twelve-month period during which the employee worked at least one thousand hours in a calendar year.

PART-TIME OR TEMPORARY EMPLOYMENT REALITIES

More than a third of all working women work only part-time, making it almost impossible to qualify under this ruling.

INTEGRATION OF PRIVATE PENSION PLANS WITH SOCIAL SECURITY

Integration allows a private employer to integrate his private pension contribution with a Social Security base. Some plans merely guarantee a *total monthly payment* of *combined* Social Security and private pension benefits.

The impact of this package approach is that when the level of Social Security benefits increases, integrated plans may decrease the amount of private benefits paid.

The table below shows how the workings of integration have the practical effect of partially or totally denying private pension benefits to workers whose earnings do not exceed the Social Security wage base.

Thus here again, women, because of their lower wage base, lose out. The integration provision allows employers to weight their pension payout toward higher-paid workers, to reduce pension benefits as Social Security benefit levels rise, and to pay little or nothing into a private pension plan for low-income workers.

PRIVATE PENSION INTEGRATION WITH SOCIAL SECURITY

Employee	Salary	(less)	Social Security Base	(equals)	Private Pension Base
A	$ 8,000		$15,300		0
B	15,000		15,300		0
C	25,000		15,300		$ 9,700
D	50,000		15,300		34,700
E	75,000		15,300		59,700

Private pension and profit-sharing plans may be confined to wages above the Social Security base.

(Here again, semantics serve to confuse rather than clarify, for "integration" seems to imply you will get the combination of pension and Social Security benefits; in fact it is a device to allow employers to see that lower-paid workers get one instead of the other.)

BREAK IN SERVICE REQUIREMENTS

A break in service occurs in any year in which an employee has no more than five hundred hours of service.

BREAK IN SERVICE REALITIES

You could lose your benefits if you have to leave your employer for any number of reasons: family responsibilities; being laid off temporarily; leaving your employer and returning at a later time.

What are the break in service requirements of your own pension or that of your spouse?

How Do You Determine Your Pension Benefits?

After you have overcome the obstacles of eligibility requirements, you will be faced with a whole new set of formulas, qualifications, and semantics to determine what pension benefits you will receive.

EMPLOYER BENEFIT OPTIONS

According to *Often-Asked Questions*, the Pension Reform Law "does not set specific amounts of money to be paid out as pensions and it does not deal with the adequacy of pension benefits—although it does require that a survivor benefit be at least 50 percent of the retirement benefit."

BENEFIT REALITIES

As you can see, there is no ruling on the amount of your pension and the benefit formula used to determine it. The Pension Reform Law still does not solve the pension problems of benefit levels and how benefits are determined.

As a result, pension benefits may vary greatly from employer to employer. Ask your employer for the details of your benefit formula.

Though there are many different formulas for determining benefits, most plans compute benefits based on a percentage of annual earnings multiplied by years of service.

Those who *work longest* with the *highest earnings* receive the largest pensions. Therefore, it is obvious that a woman has three major handicaps, even when she does become eligible for benefits:

1. She is subject to the benefit levels determined by her employer.

2. Her low wage base (57 percent of men's) predetermines a low pension benefit.

3. Women's mobility and stop-start work patterns, as we have seen, will usually give her fewer years with one company.

WIDOW-WIDOWER BENEFIT REQUIREMENTS

Does the law require plans to pay benefits to widows and widowers? According to *Often-Asked Questions*:

Under some circumstances. When a pension plan provides that a plan participant receives benefits through an annuity upon retirement, it must also provide for a joint and survivor annuity, unless the participant elects, in writing, to give it up. A joint and survivor annuity in event of the death of either husband or wife supports the survivor. The survivor annuity must be at least one-half of the annuity payable to the participant while both are living.

Would an employee's pension be reduced if the employee chose to provide the spouse with survivor benefits?

Usually—the amount of the reduction depends on the plan provisions and the difference in ages between employee and spouse.

WIDOW-WIDOWER BENEFIT REALITIES

Again the semantics can confuse you. The wording *annuity upon retirement* sounds assuring. What it means is, if your spouse dies before retirement *you receive no pension benefits*.

The survivor annuity *after retirement* is automatic, but your spouse can elect in writing *to give up the survivor annuity*.

Another mathematic semantic is that the survivor annuity must be at least one-half. Not quite. For example, a worker retires at age 65, entitled to a benefit of $150 per month. His or her spouse is also 65. Because the worker's spouse will receive the survivor annuity, the worker will now receive a reduced benefit of $120 instead of the full $150. (If the spouse is considerably younger, the reduction in benefit might be greater.)

When the worker dies, the spouse will be entitled to a portion (no lower than 50 percent) of the worker's reduced annuity benefits.

In other words, the spouse could receive only $60 of the original $150 monthly pension benefit.

ACTUARIAL ASSUMPTIONS

Actuarial assumptions are the basis of any pension plan. Employers do not make pension promises blindly. They hire actuaries to tell them the odds on how many people they will actually have to pay off upon retirement. Actuaries assume that at any given time an employer will not have to meet the total demand of the system.

The one major actuarial assumption used by the pension industry to discriminate against women is separate mortality tables based on sex. According to the sex-based actuarial tables, women are generally said to live 7.8 years longer than men. The pension industry uses these tables to pay smaller benefits to women than to men, given an equal contribution into the fund for men and women employees.

This is one of the areas in which lawsuits are pending and in which women's business and professional groups are working for change.

These requirements might seem confusing and very difficult to understand, but I suggest you ask your employer for the information which the pension plan administrator must give to participants and beneficiaries.

Your employer must furnish automatically a summary plan description in easily understandable language which must include, among other things, the eligibility requirements for participation and for benefits; provisions for nonforfeitable pension benefits; circumstances which may result in disqualification, ineligibility, or loss or denial of benefits; procedures for presenting claims for benefits; and remedies for redress of claims denied.

In addition, he must furnish you with the following:

• A summary of any change in the plan description or material modification in terms of the plan.
• A summary of the annual report.
• A statement of the nature, form, and amount of deferred vested benefits upon termination of employment or one-year break in service.
• If your claim is denied, an explanation in writing.
• A written explanation, before the annuity starting date,

of the terms and conditions of any joint and survivor annuity and the effect of electing against such an option.

• A statement, not more than once in a twelve-month period, of total benefits accrued, accrued benefits which are vested, if any, or earliest date on which accrued benefits will become vested.

I cannot close this section on the private pension system without sharing with you the entire text of the poem that opened it. The poem sums up the experience and heartbreak of many senior women.

> My earning days are over,
> 　I'm slowly going broke!
> What should have been my pension
> 　Was just a puff of smoke.
> I need to go on eating
> 　Regardless of the cost,
> Tho most of my investments
> 　Are irrevocably lost.
> My dividends keep shrinking
> 　Never to resume,
> The money they were earned from
> 　Was "served up" with a spoon!
> My doctor's bills are awesome—
> 　Costly pills I need to take,
> If things don't start to change soon,
> 　I'm heading for the lake!

I interviewed Muriel Swift, who wrote this poem. She is an extraordinary woman—articulate, sensitive, and with boundless energy. The poem was part of an article that appeared in the *Chicago Tribune*. In it, Mrs. Swift said she was "writing on behalf of the many senior citizens who share my experience trying to make do on inadequate incomes and unbelievably large outgoes." She continues, "This, of course, means resorting to one's savings, and there is no relief in sight. If relief does come, it could be too little too late.

"Many senior citizens are wondering," she said, "whether they will outlast their slender resources, and, if so, what then? Being elderly and unable to control one's own destiny is disheartening for an independent person. It is not pleasant to contemplate that the day is approaching when one will depend on dear ones—at a prohibitive cost to them.

"The absence of a promised pension has caused me to draw from savings accumulated during a working period of nearly forty years when salaries were low. Now at 77, coming from a family with a history of longevity, the future is not attractive. What should have been my golden years have deteriorated into brass.

"Today money is the key to survival, and we oldsters seem to have lost the key."

We cannot continue to accept this economic exploitation of the women who have dedicated their lives to their families, communities and business.

"Their money," not yours. *Your life, your time, your human resources—a high price to pay.*

Profit-Sharing Plans

The profit-sharing plan enables employees to participate in the profits of the employer on the basis of a definite formula for allocating contributions and distributing funds accumulated. Under the new Pension Reform Law, ERISA, class year plans (profit-sharing, stock bonus, and money purchase plans, for which each year's contribution vests separately) must provide for 100 percent vesting not later than the end of the fifth plan year following the plan year for which contributions are made.

As with pensions, it is equally important that you understand the vesting requirements and benefit formulas of your profit-sharing plan. You should know the approximate amount of your annual accumulation; when vesting rights begin, and how these rights can change. You should be able to estimate the projected cash value of your plan with continuous employment, and how your status will change with the various types of terminations.

Caveat: After one workshop, one student became aware that after ten years her profit-sharing plan totalled only $2,100 —and realized she'd be better off requesting permission to drop the plan and establish her own Individual Retirement Account.

Stock Bonus Plans

The stock bonus plan provides employee benefits similar to those of profit-sharing plans, except that the benefits are distributable in the stock of the employer, and the contributions of the employer do not necessarily depend on profits.

Under ERISA, the vesting requirements for stock bonus plans are the same as stated above in profit-sharing plans, and the vesting and benefit formulas should be examined from the same perspective.

While profit-sharing plans and stock bonus plans can vest earlier than pensions, I still recommend that you refer to earlier parts of this chapter to help you evaluate many of the similar vesting and benefit contingencies.

Caveat: Some employers allow employee contributions to stock option plans. One woman took advantage of this opportunity because the growth would be tax-sheltered—only to find the stock of her company steadily declining in value.

H.R. 10, The Keogh Act, or SEITRA
(Self-Employed Individuals Tax Retirement Act)

The Keogh Plans are qualified retirement plans that were first authorized by Congress in 1962. Prior to that time noncorporate business could set up plans for employees, but partners and proprietors were excluded from participation.

The Keogh Plan now permits a self-employed person to

contribute up to 15 percent of annual income, up to a maximum of $7,500, into a retirement fund, on maximum earnings of $50,000. A variety of Keogh pension plans is available through banks, savings institutions, insurance companies, the U.S. Treasury, brokerage firms, and mutual funds.

The employer should understand the wide number of choices of plans and conditions within the plans; likewise the employee should be fully aware of the annual amount deposited into the plan and projected benefits from the plan. All participants' plan accounts (even employees) must be 100 percent vested from the beginning. All employees with three years of service must be covered; a year of service is defined as a twelve-month period during which the employee has one thousand hours or more of service.

The same (or better) contribution formula applied to the employer must be applied to employees. For instance, if there is to be a contribution of 10 percent of the employer's "earned income," then the employer must also contribute at least 10 percent of the covered employees' full gross annual wage to the plan for the employees' benefit. The plan itself must include regulations regarding how an employee can actually withdraw his or her money under various circumstances.

You may make additional contributions to the plan account providing at least one nonowner-employee participates in the plan. Voluntary, nondeductible contributions of up to 10 percent of annual earned income or compensation, with a maximum of $2,500, can be made by an employer or employee. Any dividends, interest, or capital gains earned or realized on such contributions accumulate under the tax-sheltered plan; however, the voluntary contributions themselves are not tax deductible.

The owner-employee may receive distributions after age 59½ or in the event of permanent disability. The owner-employee must start taking distributions by age 70½. Nonowner-employees may draw benefits as provided in the respective plan upon termination of employment or reaching the stated retirement age. Regular contributions (those which were deductible when put into the plan) cannot be withdrawn before age 59½ without incurring penalties including a 10 percent excise tax on the amount withdrawn.

CHAPTER 10

"Your Money":
The Individual Retirement Act (IRA)

For millions of workers who do not have the protection of a qualified pension plan, September 2, 1974 began a new era in financial independence. Labor Day of 1974 marked the legal creation of the "Individual Retirement Account," a long-overdue opportunity for laborers to become capitalists as well.

—WARREN SHORE
Social Security: The Fraud in Your Future[1]

The Individual Retirement Account

PROBABLY THE MOST important piece of legislation ever enacted for the American worker is the Individual Retirement Act of the new Pension Reform Law. Under IRA it is now possible for wage-earners to establish their own personal retirement plans which they own and control and that continue to grow throughout their entire work lives until retirement.

With 50 percent of the American workers not covered by private plans, one of the greatest problems of planning retirement security has been not having the tax-sheltered instrument, the motivation, or the education to attain this goal. And as previously noted, few of the 50 percent of the workers supposedly covered by pensions will in fact receive them.

With the new Individual Retirement Act, you can accumulate 15 percent of your annual income—up to $1,500 each year—tax deductible. For the first time, American workers can now guarantee their retirement future under a qualified, tax-sheltered plan. A variety of qualified IRA pension plans is available through banks, savings institutions, insurance companies, the U.S. Treasury, brokerage firms, and mutual funds.

Any working individual who is not currently participating in any other Internal Revenue Service qualified retirement plan qualifies for an Individual Retirement Account. Husbands and wives can each set up individual plans. The amount saved is deducted from the gross income shown on your federal income tax return. You pay no federal income taxes on this portion of income.

The interest you earn on your retirement savings plan is also tax deferred. You pay no federal taxes on your contributions or interest until you withdraw the funds for retirement.

For women, IRA represents an even greater opportunity, because while 37 percent of working women are covered under the private pension plan system, in actuality only 9 percent of these women have vested benefits.[2]

Under IRA, many of the serious handicaps that have blocked women from securing their futures can now be eliminated: handicaps suffered because of stop-start work patterns, mobility, interrupted careers for years as a homemaker, part-time and temporary work, low wage base, and age limitations.

The loopholes, regulations, and qualifications built in by our former and present systems can largely be overcome with this new money instrument.

The Individual Retirement Account guarantees the following:

OWNERSHIP

You do not have to depend on someone else's vesting requirements to establish ownership. You have full, 100 percent ownership—full vesting—of the funds from the first day of deposit and throughout the lifetime of the retirement plan.

CONTROL

You will not be dependent on anyone else's benefit formula. The decision will be yours, and you will have full control of the plan. You can determine what money instrument you will use to best suit your needs. You will determine where you will deposit the monies, and what amount of monies will be deposited for your retirement future.

NO AGE LIMIT

Every worker is eligible, regardless of age—a vital point for the young, who have always been "regulated out" of the private pension system. They, for the first time, will have the opportunity to be covered by a pension plan at a young age and to use the phenomenal growth of money over time.

Example: If you accumulate $1,500 annually at 7½ percent (available from most savings institutions) from age 20 to 30 and make no further deposits, your fund will grow to $334,023 at age 65.

Even if you started your IRA at age 40 and continued the fund for twenty-five years until 65, you would have $116,609. Starting at 50 and continuing until 65, you would have $44,605.

NO SERVICE LIMIT

You no longer have to meet the vesting requirements of five, ten, fifteen years to establish your own personal vested fund.

PORTABILITY

You will no longer lose your pension fund when you change jobs. Your retirement account stays intact and goes with you whenever you change employment, and continues to grow even if you are unemployed.

ALL WAGE LEVELS

One of the major handicaps in women establishing sufficient pension and Social Security retirement benefits has been that their low wage base has predetermined a low retirement income. Under IRA, women at all wage levels are eligible to deposit up to 15 percent of their annual income, or $1,500 a year, and will not receive a lower pension benefit because they earn less, as with other pension plans. Their benefits will be in direct relation to the amount and number of years of their deposit.

PART-TIME WORK

Few part-time, temporary, or seasonal workers have been able to qualify for private pensions. Under IRA, they are eligible to set aside the same percentage of their incomes as full-time workers.

Most part-time workers are women. One-third of the female labor force works part-time, and this will be the first time these women have had the opportunity to build a tax-sheltered retirement plan for themselves.

SURVIVOR BENEFITS

Survivor benefits have been one of the most serious problems within the pension system. Under most past and present pension plans, there are no survivor benefits if the spouse dies before retirement. Even if the spouse dies after retirement, the benefits are minimal. As widows, only 2 percent of women receive widows' pension benefits. For widowers, the benefits are even lower. And single workers have rarely had the opportunity to pass survivor benefits on to family or friends of their choice.

IRA guarantees survivor benefits to any beneficiary of your choice. In the event of death before retirement, the full amount of the fund is guaranteed to your designated beneficiary and/or contingent beneficiary. (Rarely does the private pension system allow for a contingent beneficiary.) In the event of death after retirement, your heirs are guaranteed the full balance of the retirement fund.

NO REDUCTION THROUGH INTEGRATION WITH SOCIAL SECURITY OR OTHER PLANS

The monies from your personal IRA fund cannot be reduced through integration of Social Security benefits, as is allowable under the private pension system. These funds are guaranteed to you in full in addition to any Social Security or other benefit plans you may receive.

MOBILITY

You will no longer be penalized by your mobility and stop-start work patterns or your years out of the labor force as a homemaker. Your IRA established during your years in the labor force will continue to grow for you whether you are in or out of the labor market.

Even though you cannot set additional deposits aside in years when you are out of the labor force or during the subsequent years you might be covered by a qualified pension plan, these funds will continue to grow uninterrupted.

I strongly recommend that Congress allow nonlabor-force homemakers to qualify for this Individual Retirement Account.

This would solve many of the economic problems women have faced throughout their lives because their diverse life- and work-styles have prevented them from building their retirement security.

While many individuals and labor unions have stated that this retirement plan is only appropriate for the rich, we are talking about a deposit, a Human Life Value, of only 52¢ an hour, eight hours a day. See the Time and Money chart below.

There are several other technical points concerning the Individual Retirement Account that you should be aware of.

• If you contribute more than the maximum allowable in any year, a 6 percent tax will be imposed on the excess contribution. The tax will continue to be imposed until you "undercontribute" in a later year.

• If you receive all or part of your account before age 59½, and are not disabled, you will be subject to a tax penalty. Not only will you have to include the amount received in your ordinary income for the year of receipt, but a federal penalty tax will be imposed equal to 10 percent of the amount received.

• Under federal law, no payments can be made to you before you reach age 59½ unless you become permanently disabled. If your death should occur sooner, funds in your account will be paid to your main beneficiary. You must begin to receive payments from your account by the time you reach age 70½.

• Your account, including principal and earnings, is not taxed until you receive payments from it. If you receive your account in a lump sum, you must include the entire amount as ordinary income on the year filed or the year of receipt. However, you may be eligible to use the five-year income averaging provisions available to all taxpayers.

If funds from your account are paid to you periodically, you will pay taxes only on the amount you receive each year.

Whichever way you receive your account, however, you will probably pay less in taxes because an employee in retirement generally receives less income and pays taxes at lower rates than he or she did while still working.

If the retiree is 65 years or older, he or she qualifies for a double exemption on his income tax. If married, both employee and spouse will have four exemptions once the spouse also reaches 65.

• If death occurs before retirement and before your account is returned to you, your account must be included in your gross estate for federal estate tax purposes.

No special estate or gift tax treatment is available for amounts in an IRA.

• If you are not a participant in a retirement plan sponsored by your employer, the employer may contribute to an IRA on your behalf. Although you must report the amount contributed for you as income, you may then deduct the contribution from your gross income.

• Self-employed persons may contribute on their own behalf, if they do not have an H.R. 10 Plan, which also must cover employees.

You also can qualify for an IRA plan if you are not yet eligible for your company's pension plan. You can continue to set funds aside until you begin to qualify for the private pension plan.

Many women who are covered by pension plans and know that they will never meet the vesting requirements ask me if they could establish an IRA instead of accepting the company's private pension plan. If your coverage under the private pension plan is not a condition of your employment, you may request that your employer exclude you from the company's private pension system. And when you are no longer covered by that system, you may begin your own IRA account. If you feel that your mobility patterns in your work life will eliminate you from qualifying for your company's pension plan—and if you would prefer to establish your own IRA account—I strongly suggest you request this of your employer. Remember that your employer is allowed to make contributions on your behalf to the IRA plan.

Perhaps the most important caveat is: Carefully evaluate the money instrument you use for IRA.

Because your personal retirement fund is based on medium- and/or long-range goals, it is of utmost importance that you select the money tool that will maximize your accumulated funds.

The first decision you must make is whether you want your money in a risk or guaranteed position. If you choose a risk position with hopes of a higher return (no guarantee), you can use mutual funds, stocks, or bonds. If you want your money in a guaranteed position, you have the option of using banks, savings institutions, insurance companies, and U.S. Treasury retirement bonds.

You are allowed to make a tax-free transfer of money between different kinds of retirement accounts once every three years. See the next section in this chapter, Rollover of Pension Funds.

If you elect a safety or guaranteed vehicle and you use a money instrument from a savings institution, you will recall, from the "Time is Money" chapter, that even a 1¼ percent difference in interest rates can produce an enormous increase in the amount of the funds accumulated.

For your immediate comparison, here are the differences in the two 10-year charts.

TEN-YEAR GOAL

$1,500/year
$125/month
52¢/hour, eight hours a day
at 7½% annual rate, compounded continuously
7.9% effective annual yield

Deposit from Ages	By Age 65 You Will Have Accumulated
0–10	$1,528,290
10–20	714,482
20–30	334,023
30–40	156,157
40–50	73,004
50–60	34,129

A 7½ percent interest rate is available at most savings institutions.

TEN-YEAR GOAL

$1,500/year
$125/month
52¢/hour, eight hours a day
at 6¼% compounded quarterly

Deposit from Ages	By Age 65 You Will Have Accumulated
0–10	$631,203
10–20	339,495
20–30	182,599
30–40	96,211
40–50	52,823
50–60	28,411
60–65	8,815

These charts show you the accumulations possible from making IRA contributions for only ten years. Of course your deposits will grow to even larger amounts if you can continue to contribute to your IRA fund throughout your years of eligibility.

While only $40,000 would be insured for each account, you can establish as many separate IRA accounts as you care to have—each one in a different financial instrument, if you so choose.

If you use a savings instrument that continues to pay interest, these monies will keep growing over time, even if no further deposits are made.

However, you should be fully aware of the status changes in the growth of your account when you use an annuity or endowment contract. Leonard Groupe in his "Dollars and Sense" column for the *Chicago Daily News* explains the problem clearly: "Likewise, if you begin with the purchase of an endowment or an annuity program and can't continue (or don't want to), you will have in effect purchased a very tiny endowment or an almost too-small-to-see lifetime annuity —after having paid what would be a very high commission

—as with any insurance policy that is dropped soon after purchase."[3]

It is imperative that you read chapter sixteen, on annuities, to evaluate the other mathematical and financial snares that you will have to face if you elect the annuity contract for your retirement security. (Or, I should say, your retirement insecurity.)

As you will learn, this annuity money instrument which millions of Americans use for their retirement "security" is a money vehicle that not only leaves you with a markedly lower cash accumulation during the period of growth, but also shockingly lowers your benefit during the period of withdrawing the annuity income.

The reassuring sound of the word *annuity* becomes, under analysis, a stark example of legal pickpocketing.

The financial institution of your choice can give you additional information on the Individual Retirement Account, and the Internal Revenue Service has an excellent publication, *Facts, Information on Individual Retirement Savings Programs,* publication 590, which will answer any questions you might have.

Tax-Free "Rollover" Pension Funds—Changing Employment with Vested Pension Funds, or Changing IRA Instruments

Under certain conditions, the new law permits an individual to withdraw his entire interest in a retirement account or annuity without tax penalty, if he contributes all of it to another such plan within sixty days after he receives it. These "rollover" provisions are intended to permit individuals some degree of flexibility in shifting their investments, if they so desire. However, there is one important limitation: there's no tax-free "rollover" of amounts received from an Individual Retirement Account or annuity if there was a prior tax-free "rollover" of an amount received from another account or annuity, or of retirement bonds, within three years of the date of the receipt of the current distribution.

There is also a special tax-free "rollover" break for lump-sum distributions from qualified plans, including annuity plans under Section 403(a) of the Code, and under Keogh plans. Thus, if the entire distribution, including the cash and identical assets received in the distribution, is contributed to a retirement account or annuity within sixty days after receipt, the distribution won't be taxed.

Qualified plan distributions "rolled over" into an Individual Retirement Account or annuity are "frozen in" until age 59½. You can't withdraw any part of them, borrow them, or pledge or hypothecate them in any way unless you are willing to pay a 10 percent excise on the premature distribution which will result; and, in the case of a loan, the disqualification of the plan.

Lump-sum distributions from qualified plans can also be directly reinvested in the qualified plan of another employer, provided the switch takes place within sixty days.

CHAPTER 11

Are Women on the Fringe of Benefits?

During the past several decades, employee benefits in U.S. industry have expanded rapidly—more than twice as fast as wages and salary. . . . In 1967, according to U.S. Chamber of Commerce reports, U.S. companies spent over $100 billion on employee benefits. Scenario for 1985: The "rugged" individual who wants to take his wages in cash instead of guarantees against adversity has almost passed from the scene.

—T. J. GORDON AND R. E. LeBLEU
"Employee Benefits 1970 to 1985,"
Harvard Business Review[1]

FEW OF US REALLY understand the "plastic package" of fringe benefits that is handed to us with our paycheck.

It is difficult to analyze the value and costs of fringe-benefit coverage, since we are told—and believe—that we are "getting something for nothing."

With fringe benefits today representing over a third of our income, it is important that we understand not only the changes in the *amounts* of our paychecks but the changes in the *form* of our compensation.

Investigating fringe benefits is of particular importance to women because of serious economic waste in excessive and duplicating costs, serious omissions in coverage which pose risks for women, and resulting employment discrimination against women because of their "higher insurance costs."

Herbert Dennenberg, Pennsylvania's crusading former insurance commissioner and former insurance professor, says discrimination against women "is built right into the insurance system."[2]

There are six ways in which cost, coverage, and discrimination of group insurance can have an impact on women's economic lives.

1. Overlapping benefits, through duplicating premiums and coverage by spouse.

2. Limited coverage for women employees.

3. Employment discrimination against middle-aged women workers because of industry's higher premium cost.

4. Women left with no coverage and/or uninsurable. These include:

• Widows and divorced women left with no spouse group coverage

• Women who work in small stores and offices that do not carry group insurance

• Women whose interrupted work patterns and unemployment mean they often find themselves without coverage

5. Single women often paying for unnecessary life insurance policies.

6. Younger employees able to purchase policies at much lower rates than the group rate.

1. *Overlapping Benefits*

Where there are husband and wife wage-earners in the family, each spouse or employer is paying separate premiums, and often one spouse or both have the other covered through a family group policy. When there is a claim, each of the insurance companies pays only 50 percent of the bill—even though each policy calls for 80 percent coverage for the 100 percent premium paid by each spouse/employer.

When questioned, insurance carriers are quick to tell you that if they did not receive this excess premium, they would have to charge each employee more—verbal leverage that is sure to keep the employees calm and unquestioning. Again the employee feels he or she is getting something for nothing, so the insurance companies' profits from excessive premiums continue to increase.

When you consider that there are 20 million working wives in the United States, with the cost of group health coverage over $300 for an individual's and over $450 for a family's coverage per year, this could represent enormous wasted premiums and excess profits for the insurance industry.

2. *Limited Coverage for Women Employees*

• Some policies cover spouses of male employees, but not spouses of female employees.

• Few firms provide maternity coverage for unmarried females.

• Some firms' group insurance programs do not provide adequate coverage for pregnancy costs.

• Some women workers are not eligible for maternity benefits but the spouses of men workers are eligible.

New York's Citibank's "Consumer View Newsletter on Women and Disability Benefits" stated:

Most disability coverage is in a group plan and . . . it has been standard practice until recently not to include pregnancy in employer programs for sick leave or temporary disability pay.

This has meant that women and their families lost income when they went on maternity leave and they lost benefits from all disabilities related to pregnancy.

However, things are changing.

The Equal Employment Opportunity Commission issued its guidelines on the subject of pregnancy, a few years ago: that pregnancy, childbirth and recovery, as well as miscarriage and abortion, are temporary disabilities and "should be treated as such under any health or temporary disability insurance or sick leave plan available in connection with employment."

There are Supreme Court cases pending which will rule on whether these guidelines correctly interpret the civil rights law. If the Court rules that they do they would apply to virtually all employer plans.

Meanwhile a few vanguard employers are improving their benefits to include short-term disability pay to women staffers in connection with normal pregnancy. And many more are now providing for disability benefits to cover complications related to pregnancy.[8]

3. *Employment Discrimination Against Middle-Aged Women Workers Because of Industry's Higher Premium Cost*

Susanne A. Stoiber, in her report, "Sex and the Nation's Insurance Industry," quoted from insurance company manuals submitted to a Senate Committee in May–June 1972:

A hazard . . . for women is the industry system of "experience rating" to determine premiums. On the surface, this appears to be an equitable approach for assigning each employer a fair premium based upon the probability of accidents or sickness occurring in his particular group. The rates are calculated on the basis of the age and sex composition of the group, plus its recent actuarial experience. Women, older persons and the handicapped *do* use more health services. As a result, businesses who hire persons in these categories may be severely penalized because their 'claim experience' produces higher premiums.

Health and disability coverage are expensive under the most favorable conditions. It is unrealistic to expect businesses to give women job applicants equal consideration if this will result in higher premiums. Metropolitan Life, one of the nation's largest companies, warns prospective employers that "Claims control actually begins when an employee is hired. . . . Hiring procedures for female employees deserve special attention. Studies . . . have definitely pointed to the fact that married women are, under certain circumstances, responsible for above-average claim costs and other serious problems connected with excessive absenteeism."

Metropolitan's health insurance underwriting manual suggests that employers also consider potential difficulties such as conflicting home responsibilities and problems with transportation and child care before hiring women. "Some married women are willing to accept loss of income periodically (presumably by feigning illness) . . . rather than face up to the hardships of working full time and caring for their homes and families." The negative impact of these prejudicial comments is probably far more persuasive and influential than the modest enforcement activities of the Equal Employment Opportunity Commission—especially when they are delivered by insurance representatives who will assess a company's next premium rates.

In effect, fringe benefits have been converted by experience rating into effective barriers against the hiring of women. The economic leverage of the nation's $250 billion (1973) insurance industry is consistently used to encourage personnel practices totally incompatible with a national commitment to equal employment opportunity.[4]

The Chicago-based Women Employed did a thorough year-and-a-half study of women and insurance, and they found some interesting statistics from the same company, Metropolitan Life Insurance, in a study conducted on its *own* *employees*:

Metropolitan found that the average duration of each disability was 33% less for female Metropolitan workers (than for male Metropolitan workers). Earlier studies have shown that women suffer from acute illnesses (sudden and short-lived), but that men usually miss work because of chronic ailments (recurrent and long-lasting such as heart trouble, rheumatism, etc.).

Hospital statistics, both frequency and duration, are a major source of information for disability and basic hospital/major medical insurance. Data from Metropolitan Life shows that in 1973 its female employees had a similar or lower hospital admission rate than their male colleagues (females—87.0 admissions; males—89.9 admissions). Metropolitan Life's hospitalization study also stated that the average duration for its male employees in 1973 was 9.7 days and for females was 8.7 days.[5]

It is interesting that Metropolitan's own experience contradicts the advice Metropolitan gave employers in its former manual.

4. *Women Often Left with No Coverage and/or Uninsurable (Unable to Buy Insurance)*

Women often find themselves left with no health coverage when faced with widowhood or divorce. This is of more serious concern to the middle-aged or older woman who often is uninsurable or penalized with exclusions and riders on her health contract.

A large number of women are employed in small stores and offices that do not carry and cannot afford group health insurance plans.

Often women's interrupted work patterns and unemployment find them with no health coverage. The seriousness of the problem of unemployed workers whose health insurance is a fringe benefit that ends with their job is just beginning to surface as one of the most crucial of our health insurance problems.

This new and controversial issue is growing as the unemployment rate persists at its unusually high level. The debate is whether the federal government should provide health insurance coverage for those who lose their jobs and simultaneously lose their medical insurance coverage.

The *Chicago Tribune* reported that Congress has proposed legislation and that organized labor is increasing its demands to have the federal government institute stop-gap coverage for these unemployed workers who have lost their health insurance with their jobs.[6] The solution is complex, but it is supported by both the board of directors of the AFL-CIO and the American Hospital Association, whose member hospitals stand to lose a great deal of money if a large segment of the population is uninsured for illness.

5. Single Women Pay for Unnecessary Life Insurance Policies

Many single women do not have the need for other than minimal, last-expense costs, and find themselves with group life insurance that they do not need or want. This is something rarely recognized, but I have had so many single women express their frustrations on this subject at my workshops. I particularly recall a teacher who was livid because she was given her anticipated salary increase in additional life insurance benefits.

6. Younger Employees Can Purchase Policies at Much Lower Rates Than the Group Rates

We are told that group coverage can be obtained at a much lower rate than private insurance coverage.

This is not true, for the younger workers can in fact buy a much larger amount of decreasing term insurance to protect their families for the same premiums.

And if these workers are wise enough to purchase a guaranteed renewable major medical policy with a percentage ratio of 80/20 or 70/30 at a young age, they can keep their hospitalization insurance throughout their entire lives at a much lower premium and never be caught in the stop-gap trap with no insurance coverage between jobs.

There are new alternatives and options to the present system of fringe benefits. The new "cafeteria-style" benefit plan is growing in importance each year. In effect, this plan allows the employee to select the insurance or fringe benefits most directly applicable to his or her personal insurance needs. The employer establishes a maximum figure that can be applied toward these benefits and submits to the employee a list of company-sponsored insurance and benefit options from which the employee can choose.

This alternative was originally tested by a large group of California teachers—primarily women—who found it much more beneficial and much less wasteful to choose the benefits more suitable to their needs and life-styles.

Not all insurance carriers are underwriting this fringe benefit option yet, because they fear the higher risk involved on their own part. I strongly recommend that you negotiate this cafeteria-style option with your employer.

As you can see from this chapter and the chapter on pensions, it is of utmost importance that we learn to analyze our fringe benefits and find alternative solutions to meet our personal needs.

If we do not, the *"Scenario for 1985"* from the *Harvard Business Review* that was quoted at the beginning of this chapter will indeed direct our economic future.

The authors have predicted how the "something for nothing" syndrome and our false economic security from the "protectors" will continue to grow. It also tells us how the "protector phenomenon" has swept over the labor force and conditioned us into acceptance (taking along one-third of our paychecks), and through fear, greed, and habit programmed us into dependency.

The innovative and psychological marketing of the insurance industry has been a dominant factor in the growth of fringe benefits. Their two prime marketing tools can be very enticing to everyone: fringe benefits are tax deductible to the company (but not the individual), and we're told, fringe benefits are cheaper than we could buy for ourselves (which is true for middle-aged and older workers, but not for younger workers).

Before we abdicate our rights to our paycheck and economic security to these "protectors." I suggest we take a look at a page from a major group insurance company manual.

It instructs the salesman/agent: "How does a good pension-closer close pensions? Logic, sure there is logic. You've got a census sheet, data, tax computations . . . 33 pages of facts and figures." But the clincher, the manual stresses, is the emotional appeal to the company president: "Here is the amount of the contribution . . . that goes for your benefit . . . And here's what comes out for you at age 65. And it's a hundred thousand dollars. Cash. Tom, you could go fishing at Catalina every weekend . . . You could spend that money, because next month there's going to be another check.

"The president replies: 'I'll buy that plan, 'cause I love my employees.' Why did he buy the pension plan? . . . Because you found an individual need and desire and found a way for his corporation to pay for it. You dramatized the benefits . . . in terms of whose self-interest? The clerks, the secretaries? In terms of *his* self interest. . . . What's in it for old Dad? Bring in his hunting, his fishing, his desires, darn right. And that's how the pension got closed. It wasn't the facts and figures of the 33 pages of proposals that sold the pension."

Many of those clerks and secretaries the insurance and pension industry laughs at could be you, your daughter, your sister, your mother, or your neighbor.

Properly planned fringe benefits will have an important economic impact on your income and your future. We can change the odds by exploring new alternatives and solutions.

CHAPTER 12

Public Employee Pension Funds
(Federal, State, and Local)

The pension legislation has grown from the first person law of twenty-five years ago . . . to nearly 100 laws which are contradictory, unsystematized, and pregnant with unknown cost.

—Massachusetts Commission on Pensions, 1914

PUBLIC EMPLOYEES are one of the fastest growing segments of the labor force today. Federal, state, and local employees now represent 18 percent of the nonagricultural labor force—or almost one out of every five employees in the nation. And their numbers are growing; state and local employment has increased 20 percent in the last five years.

"In 1972, 8.5 million state and local employees were covered by 2,304 pension systems," states Robert Tilove in his book *Public Employee Pension Funds.*[1]

The primary difference between public and private pension funds is that within the private pension system the contributions are generally made by the employer, and within the public employee pension system the contributions are made by the employee—with the exception of six state and local systems which are totally noncontributory. Public employees generally contribute from 3 to 8 percent of their incomes into their pension funds.

As a result, almost all public workers are covered by pension funds, while less than half the workers in private industry are covered by pensions.

Tilove continues:

In the main, public employee pension systems are older than most private pension plans. While a few private pension plans may have been established earlier, many of the public plans were written into law—especially in the industrialized states—long before the vast upsurge of private industry pensions in the 1940s and 1950s.

Public pension systems have gone through three stages of historical development:

1. Prior to the 1920s—although lasting much longer in some states—plans were very simple arrangements, established without any idea of the ultimate cost, financed without reference to actuarial findings, often on a pay-as-you-go basis.

2. During the 1920s, actuarially funded systems were established (New York, Massachusetts and New Jersey started a little earlier). These plans generally required contributions from employees as well as employers.

3. The post–World War II boom created an upheaval in public employee systems. Benefit levels were increased; formulas were changed to accommodate to the new salary levels; money-purchase plans, career-average plans, and separate annuities based on employee contributions were generally replaced by guarantees of total benefits related to final salary. Social Security was extended to public employees, with the effect of raising total benefits. In the 1960s, some states began adding automatic post-retirement adjustments to catch up with the cost of living.

The public employee systems, however, are not without their problems.

One case that comes to mind surfaced while I was serving on Mayor Thomas Bradley's Advisory Committee on the Economic Status of Women, a committee focusing on the status of female public employees working for the city of Los Angeles. The case was reported in *Action Report*, the newspaper of Local 18 of the International Brotherhood of Electrical Workers, in the April 1974 issue. It read:

If there was ever any doubt, the issue of whether DWP (Department of Water and Power) women are getting equal treatment under the Employees' Retirement plan got what looked like the clincher this week.

A comparison study of moneys paid in and possible benefits accruing to two employees shows dramatically what the women are complaining about.

Briefly, the case of Frances Nourse and Robert B. Nourse, based on DWP figures is:

• Frances has paid $19,323.24 into the plan. Robert has paid $21,026.69. Frances has paid in 91% as much as Robert.

• Robert's full pension would be $951.36 a month. Frances' would be $369.47. *Her full pension would be only 38% as much as Robert's*—after she *paid in 91% as much as he did.*

"This is living proof that the women are not receiving as much as men," said IBEW rep Ruth Blanco.

IBEW Local 18's fight to end an alleged "pattern and practice" of sex discrimination against 2,500 women of the DWP has led the union to join in a multi-million-dollar suit against DWP management.

What's asked is that the courts stop the DWP and the Retirement Plan from requiring women to make contributions and get benefits that are not comparable to contributions and benefits paid and received by male employees of DWP.

IBEW complained in its court action that DWP *women have suffered financial loss of at least $2 million so far because of the alleged discrimination.*

The statistics in the Nourse case are retirement allowance estimates made by the DWP Employees Retirement plan.

In addition to the interesting numbers cited above, the Nourse study shows:

Frances Nourse is 55; Robert is 60. Retiring May 1, 1974, Robert and spouse will receive $171,244.80 in 20 years. Frances and spouse will get $88,672.80 in 20 years.

Frances and spouse get only 52% of the amount Robert and spouse get.

There may be many conclusions one could draw from the situation.

But the one conclusion that's not debatable is: Frances has overpaid about $8,000 into the plan.[2]

Another example of the severe economic loss a public employee can experience happened to the spouse of a professor at a state university. Her husband died, leaving his shocked widow with a pension lump sum of $17,000 instead of the $800 a month lifetime pension she would have received had he lived until retirement.

The $17,000 represented his deposit into the fund plus interest. The couple could have planned differently had the professor investigated the plan's survivor benefits.

His widow knew nothing about financial matters, not even the mortgaged status of the new, smaller home they had purchased to share their retirement years. Perplexed, she went to his associate professors for consultation but received little help.

The irony is that he was a professor in a graduate school of business.

State and local employees, unlike employees of private industry, have the option of withdrawing from the Social Security system. One of the growing controversial issues among public employees is the increasing number of state and local governments that are taking this option. In March 1976, *Barron's* reported that 322 different units of government had left the Social Security system, and 207 others had given notice of their intentions to do likewise. (It takes two years from the time of giving notice to effecting withdrawal.)

Alaska also has given formal notice of Social Security withdrawal, with Alaskan Governor Jay Hammond citing the mounting costs of the program and the higher benefits available elsewhere.

Barron's observed, in a like vein, that the four thousand municipal workers of San Jose, California, who withdrew from Social Security in July 1975 had already enjoyed a 3 percent decrease in contributions and a 25 percent increase in benefits from their alternative programs.[3]

One of the problems involved in the Social Security debate

is that those employees with ten years of Social Security deposits will be eligible for Social Security benefits without making any further deposits into the system when their unit of government withdraws.

Another aspect of the issue is that public employee pension system benefit levels, combined with Social Security, can result in public employees' possibly retiring with more income than they earned from their take-home pay. For cities like New York, where taxpayers largely pay for public employee pensions, the prospect of retirees profiting more from retirement than labor undoubtedly means future political turmoil.

Federal employees do not pay into Social Security but are covered by the Federal Civil Service Retirement Fund. The federal employees question-and-answer handbook concerning the Federal Civil Service Retirement Law, *Your Retirement System*, states that the fund "is the accumulation of money held in trust by the U.S. Treasury for the purpose of paying annuity, refund and death benefits to persons entitled to them."

This money comes from five main sources:

1. Deductions from the pay of employees who are members of the Civil Service Retirement System.

2. Contributions by the employing agencies in amounts which match the deductions from their employees' pay.

3. Payments from the U.S. Treasury for interest on the existing unfunded liability of the system and for the cost of allowing credit for military service.

4. Appropriations to meet liabilities which result from changes in the system.

5. Interest earned through the investment of money received from the first four sources.

The money is invested by the U.S. Treasury in government securities.

Seven percent of each member's (federal employee's) basic

pay is deducted from the employee's salary and deposited into the federal retirement system. An employee may pay money other than deductions from his basic pay into the retirement system to cover past service for which no deductions are in the fund. The employee may also make additional payments, known as voluntary contributions, to provide a larger annuity.

Many public employees are finally learning to do what the military has been doing for years—retiring after twenty years and going to work in private industry to build a second pension. One husband stated he quit the police force "after 20 years and 10 minutes" to take a private job.

PART IV

The Systems: Our Protectors Government Economics

•••━━◗◎◖━━•••

CHAPTER 13

Who's Dependent on Whom? Social Security

The system saves money by being set up the way it is; the more women who go to work and pay contributions, the more income to the system, and the system does not pay out as much in additional benefits as it has in the way of additional income.

—ELLA POLINSKY
"The Position of Women
in the Social Security System,"
Social Security Bulletin[1]

THE MOST BRUTAL semantic fraud in the history of money is Social Security's "benevolent" designation of women as *dependents*.

In actual fact, the Social Security system is heavily "dependent" on women as its major source of funding. Without their deposits into Social Security—for which the system has to pay few or no benefits—Social Security would not be able to function.

Social Security is able to use women as a major source of subsidy because the "dependency" designation creates a structure that maximizes women's deposits and minimizes their benefits—throughout their entire lives.

But unlike the vague and hidden "their money" of the private pension system, the Social Security cost/value is measurable. The woman worker can measure *exactly* "her money" being *deposited* from her paycheck into the Social Security system. Her *benefits*, while more complex, and cloaked in the mysterious jargon of 474 pages of the *Social Security Handbook* can also be analyzed.[2]

Social Security's "dependency" on women stems from the leveraged funding and benefit requirements—in which the odds are weighted against women's life and work patterns.

The tools and semantics Social Security uses to maximize women's deposits and minimize their benefits are ludicrous—and yet they are perfectly legal.

On the deposit side of the equation, women's dependency is not even considered in determining her mandatory deposit into Social Security.

Her deposit is uniform with that of all workers. It is based solely on her income; 11.7 percent of her income, up to a maximum of $15,300 a year, or a maximum tax of $1,790, is deposited to Social Security. (While 5.85 percent is deducted from your paycheck weekly, another, unseen, 5.85 percent is deposited by your employer.)

Now doesn't that sound like the epitome of equality?

Look again. The Social Security system inherently discriminates against women by requiring them, as lower-paid workers, to pay a higher percentage of their wages into Social Security, and by taxing them doubly if they are working wives.

On second look, we can see that a high-income worker pays proportionately less into the system. A worker earning $30,000 would pay a 6 percent tax (employer/employee) rather than 11.7 percent of the wages into the system—or a maximum of $1,790.

Since only 1.3 percent of all working women earn over $15,300 a year, it becomes clear that 98.7 percent of all working women pay the maximum 11.7 percent tax. This creates a regressive tax system under which women as low-income workers pay the highest percentage of tax into the system and receive the lowest benefit; the high-income worker pays the lowest percentage of wages and receives the highest benefit.

Look again, too, at the situation if the working woman also happens to be a working wife. She pays the 11.7 percent tax on her income in full addition to her husband's deposit. She and her husband pay up to their individual maximums of $15,300 (or a combined income of $30,600), or an amount up to $3,580 tax per family unit. (And, as you will see, the woman often receives no benefit from this double deposit.)

It becomes obvious why women's dependency status is used only in determining the benefit she receives, not in determining the deposit she pays.

On the benefit side of the equation, a woman's benefits are based on her *present* "dependency," or marital status, as well as her past income status throughout her entire adult life, in and out of the labor market.

Her years as a "dependent" homemaker are averaged in as *zero* income in determining her average benefit, and her years in part-time or temporary work are also averaged in at their lower wage base, to effect a lower benefit potential.

This clever and subtle combination of qualifications for benefits leaves most women with little or no benefit from their deposit.

The benefits women receive under the label of "dependents" from Social Security are twisted and distorted many ways in order to minimize women's retirement, survivor, and disability benefits. The most serious of these distortions are manifested in a number of ways:

1. The twenty-year duration of marriage requirement for benefits.
2. The widow's gap (period with no survivor income).

3. Dual entitlement (two deposits, one benefit).

4. Benefit formula averaging in the years as a homemaker as zero income.

5. Benefit formula averaging in part-time and temporary lower wages.

6. Earnings limitations for surviving widows with children.

7. Earnings test at retirement.

8. Actuarial reduction from taking benefits earlier.

9. Stringent disability requirements eliminating many working women.

10. Benefit loss upon remarriage.

11. Continuing taxation of widows and divorced women who will never receive additional benefits for their deposit.

12. No spouse benefits when husband chooses to work after retirement.

13. No widowers' benefits.

14. Single women and women without children or eligible children paying for survivors' benefits.

The federal government refuses to recognize the value of the homemaker—an oversight whose significance goes far beyond homemakers themselves and affects women of every age and through their changing life and work patterns: as wives, mothers, working women, widows, and divorced women.

This oversight is, of course, to the government's advantage. If women received credit for their years of labor in the home, and could continue to build their independent Social Security accounts throughout their lives, in and out of the labor market, most of these dependency loopholes would be eliminated.

The government pays the Social Security deposit for the military and unpaid religious orders out of general revenues, but apparently does not consider the homemaker of equal importance to society.

Now let's examine the impact of these loopholes, one by one.

1. *The Twenty-Year Duration of Marriage Requirement*

A woman's years as wife, mother, and homemaker have no value under Social Security regulations when a divorce occurs between the first and twentieth years of marriage. A wife is entitled to no retirement, survivor, or disability benefits if divorce occurs before twenty years.

However, the new wife is immediately covered for these benefits. The government apparently questions the economic investment of the wife of one to twenty years—but does not question the new wife's immediate value.

If the divorced woman doesn't go back to work, she will have no chance to collect a Social Security benefit. If she does, she will find her ultimate benefit to be much lower because her years as homemaker will be counted as zero income, thus reducing her average benefit base.

2. *The Widow's Gap*

If the widow has no children under 18 (or 22 if in college) she will receive *no benefit* until age 60, unless she is disabled, in which case she can collect benefits at age 50. Depending on her age and skills, she could find this a terrifying period of her life. What does a middle-aged wife, homemaker do to survive with no skills or recent work experience?

3. *Dual Entitlement*

Both husband and wife deposit into Social Security up to a maximum of $15,300 on each of their incomes. But when it is time to collect Social Security benefits, the wife must choose between taking her own benefits from her own deposit, or half her husband's benefit—whichever is larger.

Today's working woman rarely is eligible for more than half her husband's benefit—since her low wage base, zero earnings as a homemaker averaged into her income, and low earnings as a part-time or temporary worker reducing her base make it doubtful that her benefit will be preferable to half her husband's. She is thus left with no benefit from her deposit.

Dual entitlement's three areas of inequity were described

in a statement by Arthur S. Flemming, Chairman of the U.S. Commission on Civil Rights, testifying before the Senate Special Committee on the Aging. He described them thus:

"First, a two-wage-earner family may pay more Social Security taxes on their combined income than one individual who makes the same income

"Second, if the combined earnings of a couple are not significantly above the maximum amount credited for benefit purposes, the working couple may be paid less in total retirement benefits than a one-earner couple with the same income

"Third, the benefits of either the husband or the wife (depending on which earns more) are either worth nothing in terms of additional retirement benefits to the couple or are worth significantly less than an unmarried wage earner's making the same income."[3]

In her testimony before the same Senate committee, Tish Sommers gave a concrete example of this dual entitlement discrimination. A retired couple in which the husband worked averaging $9,000 a year would receive $531.80 a month in benefits (from his benefit plus an additional 50 percent for his dependent wife). But another couple with an identical income of $9,000 would receive a smaller benefit if both the husband and wife worked. If he earned $6,000 a year, and she earned $3,000 a year, their monthly benefits would be only $444.50. Ms. Sommers continued: "The classification of dual entitlement is 99.9 percent female."[4] All the years of the woman's tax deposit bring her no additional benefit.

Many wives have overcome the inequities of dual entitlement by working as public employees—in order to collect *full* benefits from their own deposits into public pension funds *and* spouse benefits from their husbands' deposits into Social Security.

4. Benefit Formula Averaging in the Years as a Homemaker as Zero Income

Benefits are based on a computation that includes average income and number of years of work. As we have seen, every year a woman spends as a homemaker is counted as zero in

arriving at her lifetime average earnings. Thus her contributions in the home serve only to reduce her Social Security benefit base.

5. *Benefit Formula Averaging in Part-Time Temporary Lower Wages*

A woman's income from part-time or temporary work is averaged into her full-time work years' deposit, thereby reducing her benefit base even more.

6. *Earnings Limitations for Surviving Widows with Children*

A widow receiving survivor benefits for herself and her children must give up a portion of her benefits if she earns additional income over the amount determined by Social Security.

Warren Shore, in his book *Social Security: The Fraud in Your Future*, cited an example of this loophole:

"As long as Mary Williams is not earning outside income and is caring for her two children at home, the Social Security Administration will send a family benefit of $651.60 each month. If, however, Mary Williams does earn money, in fact earns more than $2,760 in a year, or $230 a month, the family will lose $1 for every $2 she earns as a deduction from the Social Security benefit."[5]

Mary was subtly forced out of the labor market. Either choice, *Don't work* or *Work and have benefits reduced or eliminated*, compelled her to give up more than income. She gave up the opportunity to retrain, develop a new career, and increase her income potential. She also gave up the only chance she had to increase her own Social Security and pension benefits. When Mary is 50 years old and her children are 22 and out of college, she will face ten years with no income, no skills or career, and job handicaps of the middle aged.

She will have to spend her life taking from the economy and will be unable to contribute to it.

7. *The Earnings Test at Retirement*

According to the Congressional Research Service, "The Social Security Act, which grew out of the Depression, had as one of its primary objectives the removal of older workers from the labor force to create work opportunity for the young, and did much to establish the propriety of retiring older workers at a set chronological age."[6]

Though today we are largely distracted from recognizing the original (and present) "removal of older workers" intent of Social Security, the earnings test at retirement aspect of the law serves to reinforce that intent. The workings of this loophole cast older workers out of the work force and into poverty—in effect disposing of these "used Americans."

With over half the women over 65 living below the poverty level, additional income is necessary for survival. Yet the earnings limitation requirement functions so that when anyone over 65 is forced to work, he or she loses $1 for every $2 earned after income reaches $2,760, or $230 a month.

Every senior citizen I have ever talked to greatly resents this ruling, and complains bitterly that he or she is forced to work because Social Security does not live up to its heralded "purpose"—to serve as a replacement for earned income.

The older workers' more fortunate retired friends who receive interest, dividend, and premium income are not penalized as the earner is.

8. *Actuarial Reduction for Taking Benefits Earlier*

The Sommers Report tells us that 70 percent of women workers do not hold out until they reach 65 to claim their retirement.[7] For many of these women, there were no jobs and no other sources of income, and some were not in good enough health to withstand the demands of full-time employment.

When you retire early, at age 62, you get 80 percent of your benefits. You give up 20 percent and could therefore be giving up as much as $60 a month in benefits.

Thus the woman who is forced to collect early pays a high price for her dependency status. In the words of the authors of *Three Out of Four Wives*, "She is penalized for having made a profession of being a wife."[8]

9. *Stringent Disability Requirements*

The interrupted work patterns of women often make it difficult or impossible for them to collect benefits under the disability provisions of Social Security.

Disability requirements are more stringent than those for retirement. They require that the worker must have been actively employed in half the quarters during the ten years immediately prior to disability, or if under age 31, in half the elapsed quarters since reaching 21. This means that if a woman stops work for a time due to family responsibilities, she may lose her benefits.

10. *Benefit Loss Upon Remarriage*

If a widowed or divorced woman decides to remarry, she will lose at least part of her benefits from the initial marriage. She qualifies for only one half of her deceased husband's benefits *or* for the full amount due to the wife of the second husband.

11. *Continuing Taxation of Widows and Divorced Women Who Will Never Receive Additional Benefits for Their Deposit*

Working widows and divorced women who would collect Social Security under their husbands' benefits are nevertheless required to pay continued taxes on their own earnings—even though they will receive very little or no benefit from this mandatory deposit.

I think of the $3.72 case. After being married for twenty-five years, a woman divorced and worked twenty years until her retirement. At 65 she received her Social Security retirement benefit. Two years later her ex-husband retired, and she received a letter from Social Security telling her she would have an additional $3.72 from his account—after twenty-five years as a dedicated wife and mother.

12. *No Spouse Benefits When Husband Chooses to Work After Retirement*

If a man continues to work and receives no Social Security, his spouse is also ineligible for benefits. Many women are punished by this rule—especially those whose husbands have left them, though they are not legally separated.

13. *No Widowers' Benefit*

The husband must prove his "dependency" in order to obtain survivor benefits from his wife's deposit. Only recently has the Supreme Court recognized that a widower rearing a child is now eligible for payments made by female wage-earners.

14. *Single Women and Women without Children or Eligible Children Paying for Survivors' Benefits*

This Social Security loophole requires single women and women without children (or eligible children) to deposit a portion of their paycheck tax for survivors' benefits—even though they have no survivors who can collect. In other words, they are paying for a benefit they will never see.

The price the American woman and her family have paid for a Social Security system that maximizes women's deposits and minimizes their benefits can also be judged and visibly measured by the results of the system's forty years of performance.

Social Security's weighted cost/value ratio has left today's woman the poorest segment of our society, and the older woman alone the most ravaged. Half of these elders are living on less than $2,000 a year—with no possible way out.

It is ironic that this generation of senior citizens living out its final years in its own personal "depression" is the same generation that was forced to face the nation's Depression of the 1930s and was told (and believed) that the new Social Security system would solve the problems of income at retirement.

This "depression" is not only financial but psychological and physical as well. Perhaps that is why we have more patients in nursing homes today than we have in hospitals. They have given up, mentally and physically, with no hopes for the future after a lifetime of struggle.

But women, though short-changed by Social Security, are not powerless to change it. As Social Security's major funding source, and as a powerful political bloc, women are working through our legislative process to revise and reform the system.

Women's investigation into their exploitation by Social Security has brought many new bills to Congress—but still few changes. As of February 1976 there were nineteen Social Security bills pending affecting women.[9]

The headlines of today's papers give us further indication that today's workers—men as well as women—are becoming aware that this cost/value cannot continue or that the same fate greeting today's elders will meet them in their retired years unless some changes are made:

EBBING RESOURCES: SOCIAL SECURITY IS
ON ITS WAY TO GOING BROKE, ANALYST WARNS
Wall Street Journal
February 27, 1975

HOW SECURE IS OUR SOCIAL SECURITY?
Chicago Tribune
June 1, 1975

HOW SOCIAL SECURITY CHEATS WORKING WOMEN
Family Circle
July 1975

SOCIAL SECURITY BENEFITS NOT WORTH COST
Springfield (Mass.) *Union*
March 18, 1976

According to *Barron's*, 4,000 municipal workers have withdrawn from Social Security; 322 units of government have opted out; and 207 others have given notice of opting out.

These headlines are fostering public awareness and pressure for options, evaluations, measurements—and perhaps change.

CHAPTER 14

Empty Estates

Inheritance and estate taxes are among our oldest and also our most neglected taxes, neglected alike by legislators, administrators, and the public. Sales, income, property, and some of the other taxes figure almost daily in public discussions; but literally years can pass without a single press reference to the taxes on inherited wealth. Although the present federal estate tax is over fifty years old, Congress has looked at this tax (even perfunctorily) only once during the last quarter century.

—W. ECKER RACZ
Financing State and Local Governments[1]

THIS HISTORICALLY neglected area of taxation has eroded the estates of women for many years and only recently has it surfaced as a source of major economic waste for women.

One of the main reasons for its neglect was pointed out in a statement by William E. Simon, Secretary of the Treasury, before the House Ways and Means Committee in March 1976.

"Until recent years the estate and gift tax did not affect a large segment of taxpayers. The limited impact of the taxes was consistent with their role as devices to restrain the undue accumulation of wealth. Thus, the annual number of estate tax returns filed during the period 1923–1945 never exceeded 18,000. In 1975, approximately 216,000 estates filed estate tax."[2]

Except for the introduction of the marital deduction in 1948, the basic structure of estate and gift taxes has remained fundamentally unchanged since 1932. The present estate and gift tax rates were adopted in 1941, and the estate and gift tax exemptions were last changed in 1942.

Farm women were the first to take the lead in investigating this unfair and costly law. From the experience of family and neighbors, they found many women having to sell their farms in order to pay the taxes upon the death of their spouses.

The *Farm Journal* quotes one woman: "A farm wife doesn't know how the government discriminates against her until she is widowed or divorced. My husband and I worked hard these past 23 years to make land payments. One year ago he died at 45. Now I'm having to pay for the farm again— this time to IRS." They call it the widow's tax.

"[The Widow's Tax] is enough to turn a farm wife into a libber," acknowledges Phillip A. Henderson, Nebraska Extension economist. "If husband and wife hold property in joint tenancy and the husband dies first, the entire value of the property is assumed to belong to the husband and is subject to estate taxes—unless the wife can prove that she inherited part or held an off-farm job to meet payments or otherwise made a legally recognized contribution of money or 'money's worth.' Did the wife contribute by driving the tractor, sorting cattle, doing bookwork? Not in the eyes of IRS."

"The wife renders all these services as a part of her marriage contract," an IRS attorney explained.[3]

Women in separate property states not only find this inequity but also discover that if the husband dies first, estate taxes are paid on the property not only with the transfer to the wife, but also a second time, when the wife dies and wills it to her children.

If the husband is the first to die the property passes to the wife free from estate taxes only to the extent that its value does not exceed the marital deduction (equal to one-half of the estate) plus the $60,000 exemption.

If the wife is the first to die, the property will always pass to the husband, free of estate taxes.

In community property states, under the same circumstances, each spouse is generally treated as owner of a one-half interest in the property acquired during the marriage. The estate tax consequences are basically the same for the husband or the wife, regardless of who is the first to die.

Because of the extensive data women's groups have compiled, formal proposals have been submitted recommending changes in those provisions of the Internal Revenue Service Code relating to estate and gift taxes "to eliminate taxation on all transfers of property between husband and wife at death and on all gifts between a husband and wife during their lifetimes."

Federal estate and gift tax laws and state inheritance tax laws generally presume that the homemaker makes no economic contribution to the family.

Hearings were held on the estate tax problem by the House Ways and Means Committee in March 1976. Unfortunately, many amendments have been recommended that appear to have turned this legislation into a new loophole for the wealthy. The media reports at best are conflicting. The *Christian Science Monitor* headlines the testimony: ESTATE TAX 'REFORM' WOULD AID WEALTHY MOST,[4] and the *Wall Street Journal* headlines it: A NEW 'SOAK-THE-RICH' THEORY.[5]

When I attended the hearings in March it appeared that the predominant recommendations were to increase the estate tax exemption to $100,000 or $150,000. Perhaps by the time of this book's publication there will be more data.

State inheritance tax laws also contain serious economic problems for women. In separate property states the income-earning spouse has complete ownership and control of the assets, and unless that spouse elects to hold these assets in joint tenancy or to make them a gift to the other spouse, the entire estate is considered to belong to the income-earner, who is most often the husband.

Many women find that their years as homemakers count as nothing and that they are required to pay state inheritance tax on the entire estate after a small exemption. The state of Illinois, for example, allows only a $20,000 exemption. Therefore, if the family assets have been held in ownership in her husband's name, the wife must pay state inheritance tax on the entire estate after the first $20,000. I recommend that you read the chapter on laws and marriage for a more complete understanding of the laws of separate and community property states.

PART V

The Systems: Our Protectors
Personal Economics

⋯⋯━━◉━━⋯⋯

CHAPTER 15

The Expensive Guarantee:
Insurance

Selling practices in the life insurance industry thrive upon, and contribute to, consumer ignorance.

—PETER H. SHUCK, DIRECTOR OF THE
WASHINGTON OFFICE, CONSUMERS
UNION OF THE UNITED STATES[1]

"MORE THAN 300,000 times a day—year round—American consumers pay a bill without having more than the vaguest idea of what they are buying.

"If this were the result of flim-flam, enforcement agencies would have been all over the sellers years ago. But this is not intentional flim-flam—it is as the man in *Fiddler on the Roof* explained away so many things—'tradition.'

"These 140 million consumers—at an outlay of about $23 billion yearly—are buying life insurance policies."

So said Senator Philip A. Hart at hearings on the life insurance industry.[2]

Most of the consumers writing the checks are women, who have no idea of the economic waste involved.

Women suffer severe economic loss because of the discriminatory cost/benefit value of life, health, and disability policies and also because of their lost benefits due to lack of knowledge and improper planning.

One of the main reasons for this lack of knowledge is the attitude of the insurance industry itself towards women. One gains insight into the type of sales training agents receive in approaching the women's market from a sales training brochure published by the Research and Review Service of America titled "Selling to the Ladies." It instructs the agents:

Be prepared for some supposedly 'feminine' reactions to the subject of life insurance. For example, be prepared for the following:
• Fear of high pressure tactics.
• Inability to reach a decision.
• Reluctance to commit herself to a "long-term obligation."
• Aversion to a medical examination, objection to the bother of it and the necessity of disclosing personal information.
• Suspicion of the mathematical miracle of life insurance—because she doesn't understand it.
• Preference not to think of the future and the possible disasters it holds. (Scarlett O'Hara always wanted to "think about it tomorrow.")
• Expectation, or hope, or fear, of changing status—marriage, losing job, etc.[3]

Not only do the insurance companies insult women's intelligence but to add to the injury they charge them from 5 to 150 percent more in excessive premiums and/or they restrict benefits. The insurance industry has been able to get away with this and make a handsome profit on these excessive premiums and restricted benefits for many years. This too has changed. As women began to investigate the cost/value of their financial contracts, this economic waste became evident.

In the last few years women have compiled strong and mounting evidence of the excessive cost/benefit values, and as a result many states have instigated studies on women's insurance premiums and have proposed legislation to correct this discrimination. Women's groups all over the country have also been involved in gathering information.

We will examine separately the economic waste and factors involved in disability, health, and life insurance.

Disability Insurance

Typical of the findings of women's groups and state studies are the following from the State of Illinois. These findings evidence the many different ways that women are discriminated against in disability income. As you will see, the evidenced discrimination reflects a high cost not only to the woman but to her family—as well as low benefits to them.

SEX DISCRIMINATION IN DISABILITY INCOME INSURANCE PLANS CONCLUSIONS:

The first conclusion is that in the disability income product line there is an unequal opportunity for coverages and rates based on the applicant/insured's sex. Therefore, as this report has defined it, there is measurable discrimination in this based on sex.

• 89 (97.8 percent) of the 91 companies which responded . . . discriminated in either benefits or rates based on sex.

• 250 (32.3 percent) of the 775 responses indicated that policies available to males were not available to females.

• 503 (95.8 percent) of the 525 responses which indicated that the policies available to males were also available to females, charged higher rates to females.

• Clearly, among the companies writing disability income insurance, there is no consistency in coverages offered and in rates charged to males and females.

• Of the 525 policies available to both males and females . . . 503 (95.8 percent) contained rates from 1% to 104% higher for females.

• The 79 responding companies which applied different underwriting rules between males and females to the risk criteria and policy provisions . . . showed no consistency in the application of their various underwriting rules.

In fact, the wide variety of coverages and enormous disparity of rates for this line of insurance indicates that there are no uniform standards used by the responding companies as a whole to deal with the issue of discrimination based on sex. Without substantial uniformity among the companies writing this line of insurance, the application of the companies' business policies between males and females is at least arbitrary, and perhaps irrational.

This lack of standards results in a hardship to females: there are increased rates to *some* females, unavailability of coverage to *some* females, and unequal opportunity for substantially similar treatment among all females. This treatment is discriminatory and it its unfair.

There is no exculpation in consistency alone, especially when the effect of a company's practices is to consistently exclude females from policy availability, comparable benefits, and comparable rates.

Since there are no standards which are reasonable or consistent within this group, then all companies' policy decisions which are based on their own arbitrary standards are suspect.[4]

These findings, in addition to extensive testimony and hearings, are finally bringing about proposed legislation nationwide.

An example is Illinois' Proposed Rule 26.05 regarding "Unfair Discrimination Based on Sex and/or Marital Status." Under its Prohibited Practices Section, this proposed legislation states:

No Company shall refuse to issue any contract of insurance, certificate of insurance, notices of proposed insurance, policies, endorsements or riders or decline to renew such contract, certificate, notice, policy, endorsement or rider because of the sex and/or marital status of the insured or prospective insured. The amount of benefits payable, or any term, condition, or type of coverage shall not be restricted, modified, excluded or reduced on the basis of the sex and/or marital status of the insured or prospective insured.

Examples of the practices prohibited by this Section include, but are not limited to:

(a) Offering coverage to males gainfully employed at home, employed part-time or employed by relatives while denying or offering reduced coverage to females similarly employed;

(b) Offering policy riders to males while denying the same to females;

(c) Denying, cancelling or refusing to renew coverage, or providing coverage on different terms, because the insured or prospective insured is residing with another person or persons not related to her/him by blood or marriage;

(d) Reducing disability benefits for women who become disabled while not gainfully employed full-time outside the home when a similar reduction is not applied to men;

(e) Denying maternity benefits to insured or prospective insured purchasing individual contracts or policies of insurance when comparable family coverage contracts offer maternity benefits;

(f) Offering dependent coverage to wives of male employees while denying dependent coverage to husbands of female employees;

(g) Establishment of different conditions or benefit options for males and females. This includes more restrictive basic benefit periods and more restrictive definitions of disability to women than to men;

(h) Requiring female applicants to submit to medical examinations while not requiring males to submit to such examinations;

(i) Denying to divorced or single persons coverage available to married persons;

(j) Denying disability income contracts of insurance, certificates of insurance, notices, policies, riders or endorsements to women employed in high risk classifications when coverage is offered to men similarly employed;

(k) Offering any contract, certificate, notice policy, endorsement or rider provision which is more restrictive in basic benefit periods or definition to women than to men;

(l) The treating of complications of pregnancy in a manner differently than any other illness or sickness covered by the contract, certificate, notice, policy, endorsement or rider;

(m) The limiting of the amount of coverage an insured or prospective insured may purchase based upon the sex and/or marital status of the insured or prospective insured.

I know these lists of discriminations are dizzying in length, but I feel you should see them and examine them to understand how complex and varying the discriminations are. To further substantiate how discriminatory these differences in rates and benefits are, the Department of Labor has found that men lost 5.1 days due to sickness or injury in 1971 compared with 5.2 days lost by women.

The importance of disability insurance for the working woman cannot be underestimated. It is so important that many states, such as California, have established state disability insurance.

If you are not covered by your state or group insurance, I strongly urge you to investigate and cover yourself through private disability plans, if you or your family are dependent on your income.

As you have seen, it is vital that you compare different insurance companies' disability policies. Here are some of the facts you should compare:

• Period of coverage (one year, two years, five years, to age 65). Many companies limit the period of coverage for women to two to five years.

• Cost of coverage (premium cost). As seen above, it varies widely.

• Elimination period (waiting two weeks, one month, three months, six months).

• Percentage of salary you are eligible for.

• Non-cancellable (company cannot cancel policy).

• Any exclusions (limitations of coverage).

• Definition of disability (based on inability to perform your specific occupation—or any job).

Health Insurance—Medical and Hospital

Health insurance, of course, is important for all women in and out of the labor market. With the staggering cost of medical and hospital care today, many families can find themselves bankrupted by one illness.

Unfortunately, hospital coverage is much higher for women (up to 61 percent higher). In addition, many women find themselves handicapped by policies with "riders" and "exclusions," under which the company refuses to cover any preexisting conditions.

As mentioned in the chapter on fringe benefits, many women find themselves without health insurance after widowhood or divorce, as well as when changing jobs or unemployed. The problem is compounded for middle-aged and older women who are victims of widowhood and divorce because they often find themselves uninsurable. Many homemakers who were previously covered by their spouses find themselves without coverage at this time.

Women Employed, a group that has been investigating sex discrimination in disability and health insurance in Chicago for the last year and a half, has given excellent examples of the economic waste involved in women's health insurance:

Health insurance plans also discriminate against women. Some companies, like North American Reassurance Company, limit coverage of many medical conditions exclusive to women such as gynecological disorders and related conditions. Yet coverage for exclusively male problems such as prostate disorders is routinely provided ...

Health coverage also costs a woman more. Hartford charges a woman 48% more than a man the same age for a basic hospitalization plan. If the woman wants maternity coverage, Hartford raises her rate to 93% more than the man's. Companies such as Kemper and Washington National charge a woman enough extra over her lifetime to pay 12 maternity benefits. Yet the average American woman bears only 2.4 children according to the 1970 census.

Discrimination in rates costs the female policy-holder a good deal of money. A woman who holds disability and hospitalization insurance with Washington National, for instance, will pay $7,763 more in premiums over her lifetime (25–65) than a man holding the same policy . . .

Considering both frequency and duration of hospitalization, the average cost of female claims is less than that of males. According to the Society of Actuaries, the average claim for major medical benefits with 10 companies was lower for women than men in 1971–72. ($500 deductible, no surgical schedule maximum.)

> Males, all ages....................$1,384.74
> Females, all ages...................$1,179.26

Another report of the Society of Actuaries on *individual* hospital plans shows that women have a lower overall claim cost than men for this type policy too. . . . The phrase "sound actuarial principles" has become the industry's smokescreen for discrimination.[5]

When purchasing a major medical policy, select a non-cancellable contract (it guarantees that the company cannot cancel your policy).

Purchase a percentage contract (80/20 or 70/30) as opposed to a flat daily benefit of $50 or $100, because then as hospital costs continue to rise, you are protected on a percentage basis instead of a smaller set fee.

If possible, select a policy that does not have a limited surgical schedule.

As you can see from the above charts, it is important to compare benefits and costs before making a decision.

Determine the major medical deductible amount suitable to your needs, $250, $500, or $1,000. Remember, the higher the deductible the lower the premium. Does the deductible apply per year or per cause? And does the maximum benefit apply per cause or per person or per life of the policy?

Life Insurance: Time = Risk versus Time = Money

The basis for discrimination against women in the life insurance or annuity contract lies in the interpretation of the dual mortality tables. To understand the mathematics of the life insurance contract, you must simultaneously understand the mathematics of an annuity contract.

The discrimination of these mortality tables was validated by John A. Durkin, Insurance Commissioner of the State of New Hampshire, before the U.S. Senate Subcommittee on Antitrust and Monopoly:

Females are discriminated against in the rates charged them for individual life insurance policies. Simply stated, they pay more than they should.

The predominant practice in the life insurance industry is to charge females the same rates males who are three years younger pay. For example, the rate for a female age 43 would be the same as for a male age 40 (assuming the same plan of insurance and premium paying period).

In fact, the setback for females should be not three years, but at least twice that—six years! At the young adult ages, say 15 to 35, when males tend to do themselves in on the highways, the differential should be even more pronounced. The justification for this assertion can be proven in a numbers of ways:

U.S. Population Mortality: The 1971 edition of the Statistical Abstract of the United States gives mortality rates by age, race, and sex. From this table the following can be derived:

Male Age	Mortality Rate per 1000	Female Age with Same Mortality Rate	Difference in Years
30	1.67	38.1	8.1
35	2.21	41.2	6.2
40	3.43	47.0	7.0
50	9.30	58.4	8.4
55	14.97	64.0	9.0

Until the late 1950's the rate charged females was the same charged males, although it was well known that female mortality was lower. For example, in 1957 an actuary, Mr. L. S. Norman, commented that female mortality was 60 percent of male mortality. The rationalization for not giving females a break, prior to that time, was that they bought smaller policies and the extra administrative expenses incurred on such policies were offset to the lower female mortality. (There was also some evidence that lapse rates were lower for females, which, in turn, ought to have been an offset to higher per-policy expenses.)

We have searched the actuarial literature to find the source of the three year differential. Apparently it was mainly arbitrary. Certainly the mortality statistics showed a much different pattern.

When these same companies sell annuities to females, they use much sharper pencils. The age setbacks according to our information, are from 5 to 7 years.

In short, where it is to the life insurance company's advantage to use the full differential of, say, six years, they do it. Where it isn't, they don't.[6]

These dual mortality tables create a serious social and economic waste. This economic exploitation affects not only the woman herself but also lowers the benefits her family receives and increases the cost her employer is paying for these benefits.

According to the *Boston University Law Review*, it costs the employer about 15 percent more to purchase equal pension (annuity) benefits for females.

The *Law Review* continues:

Women, because they earn less, can less afford to purchase adequate annuity and life insurance benefits. However, even if the woman can afford to pay, she buys a lower monthly pension benefit for her money than her male counterpart because her total benefit fund must support her over a longer period of time since she is destined to live longer. When the woman retires, she may well be a "burden on society" because of her inability to purchase adequate benefits to support herself.

Whatever the economic rationale for the differences in treatment of male/female pensioners and male/female life insureds, social justice demands that they be treated equally. An elderly woman does not have less expensive needs than an elderly man; she merely has less money in the form of pension benefits with which to accommodate those needs. The survivors who receive a man's life insurance benefits when he dies have the same needs as the survivors of a woman, but there is less money for those needs. Mutual subsidization through a unisex mortality table is one way of providing equally for these individuals.[7]

You purchase insurance to protect yourself financially against early death; you purchase annuities to guarantee income for life. The insurance industry tells us their purpose is the transference of risk, and we purchase their product to guard against the risk of an early death or long life. *Fear is obviously the strongest motivating force* in both of these circumstances.

Because the sales pitch is *Time = Risk*, we forget the balancing factor upon which the insurance company makes its profits: *Time = Money*.

It is important to the insurance industry that the consumer *not* think in terms of the growth of money over time.

Herbert S. Dennenberg, former Insurance Commissioner of Pennsylvania, also testifying before the Senate Antitrust and Monopoly Subcommittee, explains one way the insurance industry twists the meaning of time:

Another misconception of whole life insurance which would be used to make a sale is: "Buy when you're young, while your insurance is cheaper."

With level premium whole life, your premium may be higher if you wait a few years, but you're not necessarily paying more, since you haven't paid premiums during the waiting period.

For example, the annual premium for a $10,000 Northwestern Mutual Whole Life Policy at age 25 is $177, at age 30 the premium is $202—a difference of $25 per year. But during those 5 years, the individual has not paid $885 of premium. Ignoring interest, it would take slightly over 35 years for that difference of $25 to amount to $885.

This particular sales pitch also ignores the fact that even though premiums are stabilized when you buy whole life insurance, the true mortality costs must increase each year as the death rate increases. The mortality costs of life insurance will be approximately the same at age 50, whether the policy is purchased at age 20 or 45.[8]

To give you another example of how the insurance industry enjoys monumental (and if you look around any major city, you'll see the monuments) growth using your premium deposits and time, examine Table A in comparison with Table B (these figures come from a major insurance company):

TABLE A ORDINARY LIFE PREMIUM DEPOSIT

$25.00 a week
$108.33 a month
$1,300 a year

Age	Ten-Year Cash Value	Age 65 Cash Value	Face Amount of Insurance
20	$12,496	$128,874	$88,909
25	12,609	99,876	77,957
30	12,756	76,800	68,089
35	12,700	57,565	58,467
40	12,347	41,467	49,123
45	11,774	28,431	40,444
50	10,932	17,947	32,502
55	10,164	10,164	25,433

Using the above table to measure the value of time, even after only ten years, without measuring any further deposits (premiums), the following example will illustrate how just your ten-year cash value amount will continue to grow *for the insurance company.*

TABLE B PREMIUM PAID FOR TEN YEARS ONLY

Age of Insured	Ten-Year Cash Value	Years of Premium Deposit	Growth* to Age 65
20	$12,496	10	$178,863
30	$12,456	10	85,359
40	$12,347	10	38,626

* Growth based on 7½ percent compounded continuously—7.9 percent effective annual yield—available from most financial institutions.

This geometric growth of money over time *for the insurance company* is in direct contradiction to the insurance industry's argument that women pose a higher risk because they live longer. The longer an insured person lives, the more the premiums he or she deposited—the more these deposits continue to multiply to the insurance company's profit.

As you can see from Table A, if you continue to pay these premiums *every year* until age 65, *this is what you would receive in return*—the insurance "guarantee":

TABLE C PREMIUMS PAID CONTINUOUSLY TO AGE 65

Age	Years of Premium Deposit	Cash Value at Age 65
20	45	$128,874
30	35	76,800
40	25	41,467

And, if you continued to pay your premiums every year until 65, you can clearly see the additional enormous profit *the insurance company would gain* from these continuing premiums growing over twenty-five, thirty-five, or forty-five years.

In addition to the economic waste of the pure mathematics of the policy, compounding the problem is the lack of knowledge women have in evaluating which policy to select and in understanding the purpose and the amount to accomplish her goals.

The first problem is: Which policy do you select? As Herbert Dennenberg's studies show, there is a 170 percent cost/value difference in insurance policies. Before selecting a policy, I suggest you read Dennenberg's *Shoppers' Guide to Life Insurance*.[9]

Women often overlook important periods of insurance coverage. In planning their estates and conserving its assets, women should understand the most effective way to hold the ownership of their husbands' policy. You should discuss this with your attorney, accountant, or insurance broker. Many women have had to pay large estate taxes because of this lack of knowledge.

If a wife is responsible for the debts of her husband's business, or if the family's assets are not in a liquid (cash available) state, insurance to provide liquidity should be examined.

Many a woman going through divorce doesn't realize that in the event of the death of her husband, child support or alimony will immediately stop. She should request that the court order an insurance policy on her husband's life or that a portion of his existing policy be transferred to her ownership to guarantee child support and alimony income in the event of his death.

If the education of your children is a factor, you might also request a policy on your husband for paying these costs.

As a working wife or a woman alone, with children or other family members dependent upon your income, you should review your personal insurance needs.

Be sure to compare policies: decreasing term, level term, whole life.

And be sure to read the following chapter on annuities before selecting an annuity for retirement purposes.

CHAPTER 16

The Legal Pickpocket: Annuities

Some people dislike the idea of a contract that might pay them an income for only a few months and then stop if they died at that time. Actually of course the life insurance company uses the remainder to provide an income to other annuitants who live a long time.

Even when an annuitant clearly understands this . . . the heirs are frequently dissatisfied if the annuitant received only a few payments and then died. It is hard to convince them that this money does not go to the company, but to other annuitants who live a long time.

—The Life Insurance Institute
Handbook of Life Insurance[1]

THE WORD *annuity* has such a reassuring, guaranteed sound. Indeed, the amount you will accumulate and the monthly income you will receive are guaranteed—to give you a diminishing return.

We have probably lost more money in this country in insurance and annuities than we have ever lost in the stock market.

The annuity monthly income concept could so easily become universally acceptable as the funding instrument to secure our retirement lives that we must begin to investigate seriously the hidden and little-understood mathematics of annuities and the semantic twisting by insurance companies (as evidenced by the quote above).

Unlike the subject of life insurance, which has been debated in Congress and extensively explored in books, information on the subject of annuities is hard to find. Traditionally, books on money management usually allot one or two paragraphs to annuities and explain them away as Sylvia Porter did in her

Money Book: "An annuity is a contract or agreement under which an insurance company accepts a given sum of money from you and in return guarantees to pay you a regular (usually monthly) income for a stated period, or more typically, for as long as you live."[2]

For many women, annuities have already become a significant part of their economic futures.

Millions of teachers (large numbers being women) and employees of nonprofit organizations are annually "securing" their retirement futures with annuities—because they offer a tax-sheltered opportunitiy and annuities are the only tax-qualified plan available to them. (Why don't they have the opportunity to select the money instrument of their choice as workers in private industry now have under the Individual Retirement Account?)

Millions of other women are also making annuity decisions through:

- Private purchase of annuity contracts
- Purchase of tax-qualified Individual Retirement Account (IRA) annuity contracts
- Taking annuities as settlement options from life insurance proceeds in lieu of face-amount payments
- Taking annuities as retirement income from vested pension funds in lieu of lump-sum payments.

To understand an annuity contract, you must look at its guarantees in terms of two different money stages:

1. ACCUMULATION: The annuity guarantees you a specific amount during a specific period of deposits.
2. INCOME: With the income stage you have two options:
   Option A: You are guaranteed a monthly income for life or a certain period, *or*
   Option B: You are guaranteed a lump-sum payment.
You should understand the differences between the two

options in terms of *control of your assets* and *the total monies
you will receive.*

In terms of *control*, you should know that once you have
elected the monthly income option and received the first
payment, you have no recourse. *The Handbook of Life
Insurance* from the Institute of Life Insurance explains it
this way: "Sometimes people ask, 'Can I stop the annuity
payments I am now receiving and get cash for the balance
of the payments?' No, once the payments of a life annuity
have started, the contract cannot be cancelled and a refund
obtained."

And, would you believe, the handbook goes on to say,
"Otherwise the plan would not work for all members of
the group."[3]

You can, however, receive a cash refund if you are not
yet receiving annuity payments.

In terms of *total monies you will receive*, let us compare the
accumulation stage and income stage using the annuity money
instrument versus other guaranteed money instruments available through banks, savings institutions, or credit unions.

As our base, we will use the same amount of money—
52¢ an hour, $125 a month, $1,500 a year—and the same
ten-year program as we have used in "Time is Money." Our
example will concern a 54-year-old woman.

Table A is an illustration of an annuity program from a
major insurance company.

Table B illustrates the same amount of money deposited
in a guaranteed money instrument from a savings institution,
bank, or credit union.

Table C compares the accumulation stage and income stage
of money deposited into annuities (Table A) or savings
instruments (Table B).

Table D compares survivor benefits using annuities (Table
A) or savings instruments (Table B).

TABLE A INDIVIDUAL RETIREMENT ANNUITY PROGRAM

ANNUAL PURCHASE PAYMENT DEFERRED

FIXED DOLLAR ANNUITY CONTRACT

BEGINNING AGE 54

ANNUAL CONTRIBUTION = $1,500.00

Optional Retirement Ages	Guaranteed Accumulation Account Value	Guaranteed Monthly Annuity
60	$ 9,755.73	$ 51.51
61	11,629.00	62.68
62	13,586.57	75.00
63	15,632.22	88.32
64	17,769.94	102.89

Monthly annuity values displayed are for 120 months certain and life.

TABLE B GUARANTEED MONEY INSTRUMENT

BEGINNING AGE 54

ANNUAL CONTRIBUTION = $1,500.00

Deposited 10 Years

at 7½% compounded continuously

7.9% effective annual yield

Retirement Age	Accumulated Amount
64	$23,336.00

Looking at the analysis in Tables C and D in terms of the two money stages, we see:

Accumulation Stage

• You are accumulating considerably more using the savings institution.

• Even with the annuity contract, you will receive more with the lump sum benefit taken out and transferred to a savings account than you would by selecting the monthly income benefit.

TABLE C ACCUMULATION AND INCOME ANALYSIS

	Savings Account	Annuity Lump Sum	Annuity Monthly Income
Ten-year accumulation account value at age 64	$23,336	$17,769 OR	Ten-year certain amount $12,346
Monthly income for life	$ 136.12* with the $23,336 staying intact	$ 103.65** OR with the $17,769 staying intact	$ 102.89 10-year certain
Age 74 total value: Ten-year monthly payments Savings account principal	$16,334 + 23,336	$12,438 + 17,769	$12,346 + 0
	$39,670	$30,207	$12,346
Age 84 total value: Twenty-year monthly payments Savings Account principal	$32,670 + 23,336	$24,876 + 17,769	$24,693 + 0
Total	$56,006	$42,645	$24,693

* Monthly income from savings institution based on 7 percent savings account.

** This is assuming that the lump sum has been transferred to a 7 percent savings account.

• It is important to note that if you stop your annuity plan, your account will diminish. If you stop your savings plan, your account will continue to grow.

TABLE D SURVIVOR BENEFIT ANALYSIS

	Savings Account	*Annuity* Lump Sum	*Annuity* Monthly Income
Survivor benefit if death occurs after *three years*	$23,336	$17,769	$8,642
Survivor benefit if death occurs after *seven years*	$23,336	$17,769	$3,708
Survivor benefit if death occurs after *ten years* or *thereafter*	$23,336	$17,769	0

• Under the annuity contract, your money cannot continue to accumulate as fast as it does in the savings account because there is a commission charge deducted up front and paid to the annuity salesman. No commission is paid on a savings account.

Income Stage

• Your monthly income will be higher with the savings account.

• Your savings account and lump sum savings account principal will remain as a permanent asset for you while paying you income for life.

• Your ten-year total savings account value will be $27,334 higher than your ten-year monthly income total.

• Your ten-year total savings account will even be $5,567 higher than your annuity lump sum total ten-year value.

• If you become ill or you need the savings account funds

for any reason, they will be available to you, whereas you can withdraw nothing from your monthly income annuity benefit.

• Your survivors are guaranteed the $23,336 savings (or $17,769 annuity lump sum) whenever death occurs. Under the monthly income annuity, your survivors will receive nothing after ten years; and before ten years they will receive only the difference between what you have received in monthly income deducted from the $12,346 ten-year certain guaranteed.

Again, the difference is in the money instrument you select. Same time period, same amount of deposit, different money instruments—drastic differences in accumulation and income.

When receiving insurance proceeds, the same principle of mathematics applies if you elect the monthly option instead of the face amount.

Similarly, some pension benefits are minimized when taken on a monthly income basis rather than a lump sum (if you have such an option).

(In both cases, we are assuming that insurance face amount payments and pension lump sums are transferred to a savings or investment instrument.)

For women, the legal pickpocketing of annuities continues.

Because they live seven years longer than men, women receive a seven-year lower benefit.

However, the insurance principle on which this actuarial reduction is based is being questioned in a number of pending lawsuits.

According to a U.S. Commission on Civil Rights report written by commission counsel Peggy Johnson, whom I have found to be one of the most knowledgeable women in the country on women's economic problems: "A charge of sex discrimination in the use of the actuarial tables appears inevitable when one considers that other facts, most notably race, have been identified as having significantly different mortality rates and sex is the only separate assumption used by the pension industry to calculate benefits."[4]

The *Boston University Law Review*'s "Notes: Sex Discrimination and Sex-Based Mortality Tables" has also stated: "The employer clearly is caught in the squeeze between insurance principles based on the concept of group averages, and sex discrimination principles based on the concept of individual characteristics."[5]

Now that you understand the economic waste of the annuity, you can see how the unfairness of the seven-year actuarial reduction is compounded by the fact that the insurance companies and pension funds pay women so much less by paying these benefits out on an annuity basis.

Be sure to read the previous chapter under life insurance to see how your annuity cash accumulation grows for the insurance company and diminishes for you.

CHAPTER 17

Giving Women Credit

Access to credit is essential if women are to be full and equal participants in this society. In particular, the economic status of women cannot be upgraded until credit is made available on an equitable basis.

—WILLIAM MOSKOFF
Associate Professor of Economics,
Sangamon State University,
*Women in Credit in Illinois: A Case
Study in Sex Discrimination*[1]

A credit manager of a metropolitan department store was asked a few years back why he refused to open an account for a woman with a high-paying professional job, excellent references, a savings account, and all the other attributes of creditworthiness. "She could get pregnant tomorrow" was his answer.

—JANE ROBERTS CHAPMAN
"Women's Access to Credit,"
Challenge[2]

"84% of the total population . . . [is] headed by a married couple living together.

—HALEY OVERHOLSER ASSOCIATES
*Purchase Influence: Measure of Husband/
Wife Influence on Buying Decisions*[3]

Over 45% of all wives work, totalling over 22 million women. Over 13 million single, widowed and divorced women work.

—U.S. DEPARTMENT OF LABOR, WOMEN'S BUREAU
1975 Handbook on Women Workers[4]

THESE FOUR STATEMENTS provide a basis for understanding women's economic role in credit.

Before we can analyze women's present and future role in credit, we must understand the questions implied in these four statements:

1. What is a woman's right to access to credit?
2. How is she limited from qualifying for credit?
3. What is her economic impact as purchase/influence agent in the purchase of products in the consumer economy and in the use of credit for these purchases?
4. How does her personal income affect the growth of the credit industry and the amount of consumption of goods and services; how does her personal income contribute to the family's ability to pay for credit costs?

Women's role in the credit economy is twofold. Their impact is vital to:

• The sales and profits of manufacturers and providers of services.
• The sales and profits of money lenders—banks, savings and loans, credit unions, credit card companies, and consumer finance companies.

But if ever the aphorism, "Biting the hand that feeds you" applies, it certainly does in the context of women in the credit economy.

Throughout American history, women have had limited access to the credit contract because of archaic separate and community property laws. *Under separate property laws,* assets are owned and controlled by the spouse who earns them; the other spouse has no legal right or interest in these assets. Each spouse has the ability to obtain credit under these laws based solely on his or her income earnings. *Under community property laws* the husband's and wife's earnings become community property in which each has one-half interest. The husband's property becomes half his wife's, whether or not she is employed. This equal ownership, however, is hedged by management limitations. Only five of the eight community property states have converted to a system of equal *management,* giving the wife by statute the "equal right to manage and control the entire community property."

Thus the dependency status of women becomes the dominant criterion for credit.

But a woman's access to credit is handicapped not only by her dependency but also by her biological role. When her earnings are considered in establishing her or her family's ability to pay—her "credit risk status" has been strongly determined by her "risk of pregnancy." With this credit requirement, a child becomes an economic handicap for a woman before it is even born.

With one's ability to earn directly related to one's ability to pay, a woman's low wages also limit her access to credit.

Thus women are economically handicapped by dependency, pregnancy and low wages.

Everyone, regardless of interest in women's economic concerns, has become informed on the widespread and ridiculous discrimination women have suffered in obtaining credit, through extensive publicity from women's groups, state agencies, and the media. The evidence compiled and published has brought far-reaching changes in both state and federal laws. The purpose of these laws is to solve the primary credit problems women have faced, as stated by Jane R. Chapman and Margaret J. Gates in their testimony before the Joint Economic Committee of the U.S. Congress on the Economic Problems of Women:

1. Single women have more trouble obtaining credit than single men (particularly in regard to mortgage credit).
2. Creditors generally require a woman upon marriage to reapply for credit, usually in the husband's name. Similar reapplication is not asked of men when they marry.
3. Creditors are often unwilling to extend credit to married women in their own names.
4. Creditors are often unwilling to count the wife's income when a married couple applies for credit.
5. Women who are divorced or widowed have trouble re-establishing credit Women who are separated have a particularly difficult time.[5]

Effective October 28, 1975, Congress changed the Consumer Credit Protection Act (Public Law 90-321) by adding "Equal Credit Opportunity" (Public Law 93-495). This provides that it shall be unlawful for any creditor to discriminate against any applicant on the basis of sex or marital status with respect to *any* aspect of a credit transaction.[6]

The new federal law includes mortgage transactions as well as consumer and commercial credit and applies to commercial banks, savings and loan institutions, credit unions, retail stores, credit card companies, government lending agencies, common carriers, airlines, stockbrokers, small business investment companies, agricultural cooperatives, and other firms regularly engaged in credit matters.

In addition the new law preempts state laws prohibiting the separate extension of credit to husband and wife if each applies for separate credit from the same creditor and each spouse is solely responsible for the debt contracted. When separate credit is extended to each spouse, the creditor may not add the two accounts together to determine finance charges or loan ceilings.

Generally an aggrieved applicant for credit has the option of pursuing remedies under federal or state and local laws relating to credit discrimination. In some situations it may be more advantageous for victims of credit discrimination to proceed under the state or local laws.

The federal law permits creditors to make inquiries concerning an applicant's marital status and to consider the impact of state property laws for the sole purpose of evaluating the creditworthiness of applicants. Also a creditor may request the signature of both parties to a marriage when required by state property law.

The law also provides that an aggrieved applicant may file suit against creditors for actual damages and for punitive damages up to $10,000. In class actions, penalties up to $100,000 or 1 percent of the creditor's net worth, whichever is less, may be assessed.

The historic growth of credit is an economic phenomenon. And today credit is one of the most significant sources of profit for financial institutions. Never since the advent of money has a single factor so greatly affected our financial and economic world. Credit has changed the habits, life-styles, and economic lives of every American.[7]

The Booz, Allen, Hamilton Report, "The Challenge Ahead in Banking," indicates the phenomenal credit growth in this country:[8]

	Outstanding Commercial Credit	Owed to Banks
1945	$ 6 billion	$ 1.4 billion
1960	56 billion	20 billion
1970	126 billion	50 billon
1980 (forecast)	298 billion	158 billion

In October 1974, *Business Week* dedicated its entire issue to an investigation of the debt economy. Their findings and analysis were staggering: "The U.S. economy stands atop a mountain of debt $2.5 trillion high, a mountain built of all the cars and houses, all the factories and machines, that have made this the biggest, richest economy in the history of the world. The U.S. is Debt Economy without peer. It has the biggest lenders, the biggest borrowers, and the most sophisticated financial system."[9]

Between consumer, corporate, and federal and local government debt, there is nearly $8 of debt per $1 of money supply. Household debt amounts to 93 percent of disposable income, with consumer installment-debt repayment taking a record share of disposable income.

To analyze women's economic role in the monumental growth of credit, one must analyze her purchase influence in the selection and purchase of goods and services and her direct economic contribution to these purchases.

There are 46 million married women making consumer

spending and credit decisions for 84 percent of the population, and 27.8 million single, widowed, and divorced women making personal and family decisions. No credit lender or manufacturer could possibly overlook the impact of these 73.8 million women.

Our entire consumer economy is in fact based on the consumer decisions of women. Not only is their impact felt through selection and purchase, but through their total time spent selecting, processing, and administering these goods.

John Kenneth Galbraith, in his *Economics and the Public Purpose*, clarifies the economic value of this time: "If it were not for this service, all forms of household consumption would be limited by the time required to manage such consumption . . . to select, transport, prepare, repair, maintain, clean, service, store, protect, and otherwise perform the tasks that are associated with the consumption of goods."[10]

Thus the labor of women to facilitate consumption is vital to the growth of the consumer and credit economy.

Perhaps it is even more important to analyze what has been and will be the *source* of money available for credit. Where did the increased ability to pay for increased purchases come from? Did it come from the increased volume of the labor market—which increased the personal income of each family? Between the years 1950 and 1970 statistics show that the increase of men in the labor force was 12½ percent while the increase of women in the labor force was 70 percent. From 1960 to 1970 alone, over 10 million women entered the labor force.

With 37.7 million women in this country today earning incomes, and 58 percent of these women as working wives contributing to family income, surely they constitute a force that cannot be ignored, whose importance cannot be diminished.

The stability and growth of the credit economy is dependent on the selection, management, income, and personal responsibility of women.

Women's credit decision-making in the business world is also rarely evaluated or understood. The first to recognize this were the credit card companies. BankAmericard, Master Charge, American Express, and airline credit card companies have been fully aware of who makes the decisions for airline, hotel, and luncheon reservations—and who makes the office purchases.

Business Week reported: "A growing number of retailers, credit card companies, and bankers have been courting women as ardently as any young lover. One big attraction: the burgeoning financial clout of the female market, which promises to become an important consumer segment all by itself."[11]

If all the women making personal and business financial decisions decided to use Master Charge instead of Bank-Americard as their credit card choice, I wonder what the economic impact on the credit card industry would be.

My most serious concern for women is that they understand the economic waste involved in the improper use of the credit tool. I have seen the progressive debt syndrome destroy families.

We are bombarded everywhere by enticements to spend our money, through television, newspapers, billboards—every form of media. It seems so easy to buy now and pay later. The deferred pain and instant satisfaction can so easily become a habit, as any debt or family counselor can attest. I have seen that plastic card create an almost narcotic dependency. I cannot enumerate the many women who have told me of their difficulty or inability to control credit purchases. Many have told me how their credit limits have automatically been increased—and how they find themselves becoming indebted for these increased amounts.

The best advice I can give anyone who finds herself in this trauma is either to tear up her cards and purchase strictly on a cash basis, or give her credit cards to a trusted friend or family member who will hold them for her until she can get this habit-forming pattern under control.

Another serious area of concern is the enormous credit debt that faces our young people or their parents in funding a college education.

Many young people are graduating from college and entering their professional lives $5,000 to $15,000 in debt. If they marry and their spouse also has a student-loan debt to repay, the young couple can start out with almost insurmountable economic handicaps. Next to the purchase of a home, this has become one of the largest debts today's young people are facing. Where the families have absorbed all or part of these costs, the parents also suffer difficult financial setbacks if they are at a time in their lives when they are anxious about setting money aside for their own retirement future.

Finding alternative ways of funding this debt to maintain quality education should be one of our most serious economic concerns.

While years ago families could plan ahead and save for their children's college expenses, today education-by-debt has become almost inevitable. This is due in part to the exorbitant costs of education. But it relates also to the complex factors that control our economic lives and make it nearly impossible for us to save. As you saw in the preceding chapters on business and government economics, our inability to save is closely related to the paycheck leakage that drains away 40 to 50 percent of our income.

PART VI

The Future: Women's Changing Life-Styles

···━━◉◉◉━━···

CHAPTER 18

Laws and Marriage

Any woman who studies the details of marriage law will be appalled at what she is getting into, because the fact is that she loses a great number of her rights.

—DR. WILLIAM J. GOODE
Professor of Sociology,
Columbia University
*Social Change and
Family Renewal*[1]

The protection for the woman which state-regulated marriage is said to provide is often more illusory than realistic. In actuality, many thousands of husbands (and an increasing number of wives) annually desert their spouses despite the sanctity of both governmental and religious marriage services.

—SIDNEY M. JOURARD
*Reinventing Marriage:
The Perspective of a
Psychologist*[2]

LAWS, LOVE, AND MARRIAGE really do go together like a horse and carriage. But, unfortunately, when a crisis occurs, the woman often finds herself like a horseless carriage—unable to move ahead with her personal and economic life.

Few men or women are aware of the marital laws that control their lives.

According to Anne K. Bingaman, attorney and noted authority on marriage and divorce law, "On the day a woman marries, her financial situation is altered drastically by the marital property law of the state in which she and her new husband reside. If they live in one of the forty-three *separate property* jurisdictions, her financial rights and responsibilities in the marriage, upo̧ divorce, or upon her death or her husband's death, will be governed by laws which are essentially the altered remnants of the English common law much as it existed soon after the Norman Conquest.

"If she and her husband reside in Washington, California, Arizona, New Mexico, Texas, Louisiana, Nevada or Idaho, the new wife's financial rights at all stages of her life will be governed by the marital property system known as *community property*, older yet than the common law system, and also substantially altered by legislative reforms."[3]

Under *separate property laws*, the earnings of each spouse after marriage retain precisely the status they had before marriage as the separate property of the earning spouse, in which the other has no legal right or interest. Each has the right to contract with regard to those earnings, obtain credit based upon them, and manage and control them. All property brought to the marriage or inherited is the separate property of the owning spouse and under his or her sole management and control.

Under *community property laws*, the husband's and wife's earnings become community property, in which each has one-half interest. The husband's property becomes half his wife's, whether or not she is employed. Each spouse retains as his or her separate property any property brought to the marriage or inherited during it, unless it is commingled. Community property laws become more confusing when it comes to management of property.

"Until 1972," says Anne Bingaman, "no community property state allowed wives to manage community personal property equally with their husbands, although some did allow them to manage their own wages. Since 1972, however, five of the eight community property states have converted to a system of equal management, giving the wife by statute the 'equal right' to manage and control the entire community personal property. In Texas, a wife may control her own earnings and may jointly control the community property if her earnings are commingled with her husband's. In Nevada and Louisiana, a wife's right to management and control remain restricted or non-existent."

Despite all the discussions on new life-styles and future family structures, marriage is still the most important economic unit of our society—and it is doubtful that this economic and social significance will change in the future.

Marriage is an economic partnership, affecting not only the individuals involved but impacting the whole of the American economy. There are over 46 million married couples living together in the United States, who as family units represent 84 percent of the total population.

But marriage is an unusual partnership—because while both spouses share the family responsibilities, only one, the income-earner, controls the financial ownership of the partnership, under the laws of all but the eight community property states.

Unfortunately, many women are under the illusion that wives enjoy many financial rights, including the right to be supported by her husband—in exchange for providing the wifely services of keeping the house and caring for any children the couple may have.

Actually, the only financial right of a wife who is not employed is the support of her husband in the fashion and manner *he* chooses for her. I know of no case where a court has intervened in an ongoing and happy marriage to determine the exact fashion and manner of support. In other words, a husband's duty of support is *totally unenforceable* under the marriage laws.

A wife has no legal interest or right to her husband's earnings or what those earnings purchase, unless he deliberately makes a gift to her of some portion of his property by placing it in their joint names or in her name alone.

In essence, the federal government and the forty-three separate property states have so declared that the life, work, and dedication of a woman working unpaid in her home is of no value under state or federal law. A wife's limited access to ownership, contracts, property, and inheritance creates extreme handicaps in planning her economic future. Because of these financial laws, she faces difficulty in the following areas:

• The distribution of property upon the termination of marriage by widowhood or divorce.

• The distribution of property by will, gift, bequest, or sale during her marriage.

• The availability of credit.

These laws have created economic tragedies for those women who have rich and fulfilling marriages, for those who have suffered through widowhood and divorce, as well as those in ongoing marriages whose husbands have deliberately excluded them from financial partnership.

For *divorced* women: How can you measure the economic loss or psychological fears of a woman who is divorced after many years of married life? Often she leaves her marriage with little or nothing. Statistics show that only 14 percent of divorced women are awarded alimony, and that only 46 percent of those collect alimony regularly. Because custody of children is generally awarded to mothers, many of these women are left with children to support. Today 6.8 million families are headed by women. Statistics also show that only

44 percent of all divorced women receive child support, and only 47 percent of those are collecting such support regularly.[4]

The rarely seen or discussed but often experienced *marital relationship in which the husband uses his ownership of assets to limit and control his wife* is a very serious problem. Many homemakers have dedicated their lives to their families, but live in fear because they know there is no way they can build their own personal economic lives—even though the family assets may be substantial. These women die penniless, with no property whatsoever to leave to their children, their parents, or other loved ones, unless they are fortunate enough to have inherited their own money or property.

Even in widowhood, the husband's financial control continues beyond the grave in separate property states—for he is able to decree that his wife receive only a limited amount of the family assets.

According to the Bingaman Report: "In those jurisdictions where a form of common-law dower is still in effect, the wife has the right to a life estate interest in an amount varying from ⅓ to ½ of the real property which her husband either owned at any time during the marriage or died owning. A dower interest is only the right to enjoy the property or its benefits *for the lifetime of the surviving wife* [italics added], not an absolute ownership interest. The deceased husband has the right to name those persons who will take the property after the wife's death.

"In those states having a 'widow's election,' also known as a 'forced' or 'non-barrable' share of the deceased husband's estate, the wife is given an absolute ownership interest in ⅓ to ½ of all the husband's property which he owned at the time of his death, regardless of any provision in his will to the contrary."

Saddest of all is the *widow* who has always been told "not to bother her pretty little head" or "think about such things" as financial matters by a loving and protective husband. Upon his death she finds herself in a financial nightmare of taxes, laws, and documents that she rarely comprehends. It is usually then that she finds her years as a homemaker have counted for nothing in the eyes of state and federal governments, and she is subjected to exorbitant taxes because of lack of knowledge or planning. She has rarely thought of her life alone, or how she would get by with or without income during this difficult period of transition.

The economic waste effected by the tragic situations of these women is beyond measure.

Surprisingly, most of the families I have encountered simply don't realize the impact of marriage and ownership laws on their economic futures. These husbands and wives, with rich and fulfilling marriages, often create their own tragedies inadvertently. Though husbands have no intention of cutting their wives out of assets or ownership, by their lack of knowledge—and financial patterns that have become a habit —they have arranged their affairs in ways that the state and federal laws will heavily penalize them.

Most men who have been able to acquire assets become quite enraged when they realize the high taxes that will be taken from their wives and estates upon their deaths. Often they first become aware of this through the death of a family member or friend.

For a full explanation of the marital property laws of your state, I suggest you contact your attorney.

Many women's groups as well as the Homemaker Committee of the National Commission on the Observance of International Women's Year are recommending amendments of federal and state estate, inheritance, and gift laws to eliminate such taxes in transfers of property between spouses.

Be sure to read the chapters on the merry widow and empty estates for further tax and planning information.

Within marriage it is crucial that spouses open lines of communication with each other in order to discuss all financial matters objectively. A note of caution, however. Financial matters approached with hostility will cause much family dissension. It is vital to enter into the subject with a spirit of cooperation in order to learn how to conserve and distribute the assets each of you has worked your lifetime to accumulate.

CHAPTER 19

The Spoils: Divorce

Facade of protection: Changing divorce laws are a case in point. The tragedy of the new "liberal" no-fault laws, especially those which allow either partner to terminate the marriage at will, is that they superimpose a legal facade of equal protection upon very unequal situations.

—Tish Sommers
"The Compounding Impact
of Age on Sex"
Civil Rights Digest[1]

The "great divorce debate" today centers on who is to blame for our soaring divorce rate.

Indeed it is soaring—the divorce rate doubled between 1960 and 1973, and today 455 out of every 1,000 marriages ends in divorce. There are 3.6 million divorced women in this country. Divorce is so prevalent that it has become a news "beat." A small, biweekly newspaper in rural Illinois, the *Hillsboro and Montgomery County News*, now runs a "Divorce News" column—which is longer than the "Wedding Bells" column.

The fingerpointing begins with judges and lawyers, who are quick to cite "the women's lib movement" as "responsible for soaring divorce rates." So said Judge Beatrice Mullaney, a 69-year-old retired judge from Massachusetts who handled more than ten thousand divorce, separation, and custody cases during her nearly twenty years on the bench.[2]

A San Francisco judge was also quick to blame women's liberation: "We're taking women at their word. They say they don't want anything from men."[3]

A Chicago divorce lawyer, David B. Carlson, states: "The economic impact of the women's movement on divorce laws and interpretation of existing laws certainly has been more in favor of men than women."[4]

These statements and like ones by judges and lawyers have convinced many women seeking divorce that "these women's libbers have taken away the rights we have had under the law." They feel they will, in fact, receive less support from their husbands because of the women's movement.

Nothing could be further from the truth. Today the consequences of no-fault divorce laws are among the major concerns of women dedicated to social, economic, and cultural improvement of women's lives.

Tish Sommers, a woman dedicated to the needs of the Displaced Homemaker (the middle-aged woman left alone by divorce or widowhood), states:

A factor adding to the growing number of nonmarried (separated, divorced, widowed, or single) in the older population is the increase of divorce especially in "no-fault" States. In these no-fault States the risk of divorce in later years has been dramatic. In Nebraska, within six months after the new law went into effect in 1962, a 59.4 percent increase in divorces occurred among those married 31 years or more; a 49.5 percent increase among those married 26 to 30 years; and 18.2 percent increase among those married 16 to 20 years.

The Committee on the Homemaker of the National Commission on the Observance of International Women's Year 1975, chaired by former Congresswoman Martha Griffiths, has recommended that the state, county, and city commissions on the status of women, and other organizations concerned with the welfare of children and dependent spouses, actively seek amendments in state divorce laws where necessary, to assure that as a minimum the economic protections for dependent spouses and children of the Uniform Marriage and Divorce Act are included.

In its report this committee further explained the history of no-fault divorce:

The Growth of No-Fault Divorce: Prior to 1933 all the States in the United States permitted divorce only for serious fault on the part of one of the spouses. The trend toward easier divorce began in 1933 when incompatibility became a ground for divorce in New Mexico. Divorce after a period of separation, introduced shortly thereafter, was permitted in 21 States by 1961.

This trend has been greatly accelerated by the promulgation in 1970 of the Uniform Marriage and Divorce Act by the National Conference of Commissioners on Uniform State Laws, which provides only one ground for divorce, "irretrievable breakdown" of the marriage. The National Conference, a body formed in 1892, which is very influential in legal circles and State legislatures, is made up of representatives from each State appointed by the Governor.

The growth of no-fault divorce, *without concurrent changes in provisions for division of property, alimony and child support, has eroded the economic protection of dependent spouses and children, which has always been minimal in most cases* [italics added].

Contrary to common belief, alimony has been granted only in a very small percentage of cases, and fathers by and large are contributing less than half the support of children in divided families; furthermore, alimony and child support awards are very difficult to collect.

A poll of 1,522 women conducted by this Commission indicated that only 14 percent of divorced wives are awarded alimony and only 46 percent of those collect it regularly. Only 44 percent of divorced mothers are awarded child support; and of these only 45 percent are collecting regularly.

The common belief about large and frequent alimony and child support payments has apparently arisen because of publicity about a small percentage of cases arising under the fault system. Under that system a husband is sometimes willing to make a more generous settlement than a court would allow because he wants to avoid the publicity of a contested case or he needs the cooperation of the dependent spouse in procuring the divorce. Under the fault system, a dependent spouse has some leverage in securing better economic arrangements than the very inadequate arrangements usually made by the courts. This leverage is lost or seriously eroded by legislation providing for no-fault divorce at the option of one party. . . .

Sections of the law relating to division of property, maintenance, child support, child custody and enforcement (the economic provisions) *strengthen* [italics added] the rights of homemakers and children.

Most States adopting the "irretrievable breakdown" grounds of the Act *have not adopted the economic provisions* [italics added], however. None of the States having separation or incompatibility as their "no-fault grounds" have adopted the economic provisions. Only five States now have only fault grounds. For example, of the 46 States having some form of "no-fault" divorce, only 9 recognize the "contribution of the homemaker" as a factor to be considered in economic arrangements at divorce.

One of the states now working to improve the status of the homemaker is New York. In March 1976 a bill was introduced in the New York legislature which would, among other things, recognize the contributions of the homemaker to the marriage or contributions to career or career potential.[5]

The chairman of the New York County Lawyers Association Committee on Matrimonial Law explained, "The wife of a corporate executive who stays home and minds the children and entertains to aid her husband's advancement would be considered a factor in the husband's success. Her contribution would be given an economic value by the court."

The homemaker's contribution would be part of the considerations courts would use to "mandate an equitable division of the assets of a marriage," the *New York Times* reported.

The two major economic questions involved in any divorce are property and income: (1) the property division, and (2) income from the payment of alimony and child support.

The debate over which offers the greatest security and advantage to the wife is very confusing. The press is quick to say that when there is a property settlement it is advantageous to the husband and detrimental to the wife.

The Bingaman Report points out why property division *could be more advantageous* to women: "With alimony and child support orders elusive promises at best, the matter of property division at divorce is one of paramount interest to wives in the United States."[6]

She validates this with a further statement:

Although it is common belief that alimony awards are a component of most divorces, that belief is simply unfounded. In fact alimony is awarded in less than 10 percent of all divorces, and because alimony is deductible from the husband's income and includible in the wife's, payments which are actually for the support of children are often labelled "alimony" to lower the husband's income tax. Thus, alimony is not a large factor to be considered in the property questions which arise upon divorce.

Child support, which is customarily awarded to a wife granted custody of children, is not as customarily paid.

The record of child support payments actually made by husbands is a dismal one, as demonstrated by the following statistics: 62 percent (of husbands) fail to comply fully with court ordered child support payments in the first year after the order, and 42 percent do not even make a single payment. By the tenth year, 79 percent are in total noncompliance.

Thus, with alimony awards infrequent and child support awards difficult or impossible to enforce, the question of the division of property owned by either spouse upon divorce is a crucial one for wives.

The nonpayment of child support has been an important factor in the increase of families living in poverty. "Women are the primary victims of poverty," according to Dr. Barbara Bergmann of the University of Maryland's Department of Economics and leading authority on women's role in the economy. She continues: "One third of the poverty families are headed by women."[7] The U.S. Commission on Civil Rights' June 1974 report, "Women and Poverty," states: "There has been an increase of 33 percent of female-headed families living in poverty in the last decade."

Shockingly, many of these families living in poverty are the ex-wives and children of affluent fathers, according to the Rand Corporation report written by Marion P. Winston and Trude Forsher entitled, "Non-Support of Legitimate Children by Affluent Fathers as a Cause of Poverty and Welfare Dependence." The report noted that "social workers and police investigators verified that children of many physicians, attorneys and other $25- to $30,000 a year men are on Aid for Families with Dependent Children."[8] Thus the ultimate funder of this child support is the taxpayer.

Many other women supporting their children and struggling to stay off Welfare are also victims of the nonenforceability of court-ordered child support. In researching the impact of the new parent locator system (set up to track down non-paying fathers of Welfare recipients), I was told by that office that eight out of ten calls they receive are from women not on Welfare looking for their ex-husbands who had disappeared and stopped paying child support.

New laws solve some problems and create others. New York and some other states are working to incorporate "homemaker contribution" and "equitable division of assets" provisions into divorce reform legislation.

But, as we have seen, in most states the no-fault *grounds* have been adopted, but the *economic responsibilities* have not. The usual case has been that states have adopted the Uniform Marriage and Divorce Act's grounds for an "easy out" for husbands but *have failed* to adopt UMDA's companion provisions for spouses' economic responsibilities. These are made explicit under Section 307 of the act, which states: "Upon divorce . . . all property, regardless of the name of the spouse in which formal legal title is held, shall be divided between the spouses according to such factors as the duration of the marriage, the skills and employability of each spouse, and the age, health, and station in life of each." The section thus specifically includes the contribution of a spouse as a homemaker as a factor to be considered in the division of property belonging to both spouses upon divorce.

But in most states division of property upon divorce *still follows the archaic laws* of separate property and community property. Theoretically, in a separate property system, the spouse who has earned property is the sole owner of it. In those marriages—over 55 percent of all marriages—in which the wife does not work outside the home, the spouse who owns property upon divorce will necessarily be the husband. Even in those marriages where the wife is employed, the property she has accumulated is sure to be of less value than her husband's, because of women's lower pay scales and the years even most employed women spend outside the labor force rearing children.

Theoretically, then, upon divorce, property is divided according to which of the spouses owns it. Obviously the separate property system gives a husband much-favored odds.

In community property states, although the statutes give each spouse a vested ownership interest in one-half of all community property, only two of the eight states require that such property be divided equally upon divorce. In the six other states, the statutes allow a court in a divorce proceeding to make such division of the community property as it considers "equitable" under the circumstances.

In particular cases, such statutes may work a hardship upon the wife, particularly in those states where fault is taken into consideration in dividing property upon divorce. But in the majority of situations the wife in a community property state is aided by the unstated presumption that community property belongs equally to the spouses, and should be divided equally upon divorce.

Upon divorce, then, while the differences between the two

systems may be in fact less great than they are in theory, the basic premises of the separate and community property systems have a substantial effect on the divisions of property ordered.

The prevalence—and public tolerance—of divorce today tends to blind us to the personal crises involved. Divorce is one of the most serious crisis changes a woman can experience in her life. Whatever her age, the dissolution of her marriage brings great emotional upheaval and casts her out into the world alone, faced with the challenge of developing a new life and finding solutions to everyday problems.

She is generally faced with the problem of building her economic security from scratch, and she finds this problem is compounded by systems and laws that have accorded her no economic value.

With divorce becoming a growing economic and social contingency, it becomes obvious that we must find new ways and establish new laws and systems that will enable each person to build his or her economic life on a sound and continuing basis.

CHAPTER 20

"Truly" Single

When I was a young girl, I imagined I'd grow up to marry a doctor and walk down Michigan Avenue in fancy clothes and smoke imported cigarettes. Now I'm single and a clerk on Michigan Avenue, and I have problems affording a polyester pants suit.

—"For Singles, Life Isn't All 'Swinging'"
U.S. News and World Report,
December 8, 1975[1]

SINGLE WOMEN make substantial contributions to today's labor force and the economy. We see the often-cited statistic that there are 27.8 million single women in this country, but we rarely see this figure broken down by true marital status.

For "single" in many demographic descriptions is the term for anyone not maritally connected. It includes widows, divorced and separated women, and the never-married.

The never-married woman resents this kind of "lumping" with other groups, for her problems are usually completely different. For the purpose of analyzing the economic concerns of the never-married woman, this chapter will be devoted to the "truly" singles.

The demographics show that as of 1974 there were 14.3 million single women in the adult population (making up 18.4 percent of all adults). There are 8.2 million of these women in the labor force (making up 23.3 percent of all workers). Moreover, the average single woman spends as many years in the labor force as men—forty-five years of her life.

One is not surprised to see that 71.5 percent of all single women ages 20–24 work nor that 82.8 percent of all single women ages 25–29 are workers. But similar percentages apply as we go up the age scale.

79.6 percent of all single women ages 30–34 work;

72.5 percent of all single women ages 35–44 work;

77.7 percent of all single women ages 45–54 work:

64.3 percent of all single women ages 55–64 work, and, even after the cutoff retirement age of 65, 33.9 percent of all women 65 and over are members of the labor force.[2]

"Single" in the popular mind also carries the erroneous connotation of "swinging." Our common stereotype links "single" with "young."

Today the stigma of being single has lost much of the power it once carried, but its memories linger on. History and literature abound with pejorative expressions connected with the single state: "old maid," "maiden aunt," and "spinster" (the word *spinster* came about when, in the early days of American history, the excess populace of women who had to depend on themselves for support took jobs at the spinning wheels in the cotton mills).

For many years, single women have suffered many forms of legal discrimination in addition to intense societal pressure to marry. Parents, often anxious for grandchildren, have nagged them toward nuptials. Friends, relatives, and colleagues often have regarded them as kinds of freaks for failing to go along with what one single woman called "the Noah's Ark Syndrome, the assumption that two by two is the American way of life." Single women have been regarded as just biding time until "the right man comes along."

The prevalence of this "pairing pressure" has made single women's economic lives particularly difficult in three areas:

- Jobs
- Credit
- Housing

Concerning *jobs*, many employment practices institutionalize society's attitude that singlehood is simply an inter-

lude before marriage. Thus singles have a harder time getting
hired, getting equal pay, getting raises and promotions.

Some employers steer away from hiring singles because
they regard them as more "temporary" (waiting to find the
right man), therefore less stable, therefore less desirable. Since
there is no law prohibiting discrimination on the basis of
marital status, employers have in the past been quite blatant
in telling employment agencies to look for "marrieds only."

Even when hired, singles often get shortchanged when it
comes to pay and raises. One young women in her middle
thirties told me of a former boss who paid her $11,000 a
year less than the three male department heads with whom
she shared equal status on the organizational charts. "He said
I didn't need as much money as the men, since I didn't have
a family to support," she recalled. "My reply was that my
economic needs were as great as theirs, and it wasn't my
fault that I didn't have a husband to supplement the family
income, as those men's wives supplemented their family
incomes."

These attitudes are slowly changing. According to the *Wall
Street Journal*, some workers now think being single is an
employment asset. A female middle manager on the West
Coast found that being single "frees you to spend the time a
woman is expected to spend to get ahead." A woman in a San
Francisco securities firm said, "The company seems to think
you're a lot more serious about your job if you aren't
attached." The single state also allows for more travel, a
prerequisite for some positions and promotions.

As employer attitudes shift, "behavior away from work
seems of little concern to employers," the *Journal* adds. "As
long as your work gets done, they don't care what you do
outside the office," a single girl told the newspaper. One
corporation official "attributes the easing of corporate attitudes
to 'a phenomenal increase among working women who are
also breadwinners.' "[3]

Singles in the business world also often find that their jobs

come prepackaged with benefit packages more appropriate
to married couples. To collect fringe benefits more suited to
singlehood, take note of the following:

1. Ask your employer if you may have the option of
cafeteria-style benefits—so that you get (and if your plan
is contributory, will only have to pay for) just those benefits
best suited to your needs and life-style. See the chapter
on fringe benefits for further information.

2. Check on your company's health and disability policies.
If you do not have group insurance, make sure you have
made private arrangements. And, if you are young, you may
find private major medical and disability insurance is less
expensive for you than a group plan. Since you will have no
one but yourself to fall back on, be sure you are *well covered*
in the event of illness or disability. Review the chapter on
health and disability insurance.

3. Investigate the vesting requirements of your company's
pension plan. Make sure that you understand the vesting
regulations and the benefit formulas. Review the chapter on
pensions to evaluate whether you will in fact qualify for your
pension plan. If you will not, retirement planning should be
one of your prime economic goals.

4. If you work for a company not covered by a pension
plan, you would qualify for the Individual Retirement Account, which allows employed pensions not covered by a
pension plan to set aside up to $1,500 a year tax free.

If you are covered by a pension plan but feel you will not
qualify for this benefit because of your work patterns, you
could ask if your employer can legally exclude you from the
plan and set up your own Individual Retirement Account.
See the chapter on IRA for more information.

Credit was probably the single woman's greatest bugaboo
until passage of the Equal Opportunity in Credit Act of 1975.
Until this bill outlawed discrimination on the basis of sex
or marital status in granting credit, single women were often

denied credit even though they could prove ability and willingness to repay a loan. Credit card companies, mortgage issuers, department stores, and banks historically regarded single women as less stable financially than their married counterparts. This prejudice still lingers in some quarters.

Housing is a field closely tied to credit, and single women's problems in obtaining credit in the past limited their access to renting or buying the housing of their choice. Until the new credit law (mentioned above) was passed, singles found getting a loan to obtain housing virtually impossible. Moreover, bankers often assumed that a woman alone couldn't maintain the value of a house because she would be "unable" to make improvements and maintain upkeep—even though many family homeowners pay for such work and don't perform these tasks themselves.

(The easing of prejudice has meant the number of single women in the market for homes has soared in the past five years. One Boston mortgage company executive recently reported sales of homes for single women had gone from zero to one thousand since 1970.)

In housing, being single has often meant sleeping on a studio bed—as the single alone could afford no more. Many singles still ease their economic burden of rent by doubling up.

Today, most of "the discrimination facing single women . . . is less violent than it was a decade ago," according to Dr. Gunhild Hagestad, assistant professor in the Department of Behavioral Sciences at the University of Chicago, who has made a study of single women. "This is due in part to the growing numbers and growing economic and political power of singles. The number of single women over the age of 24 has doubled in the last few years. . . . Demographers believe many single women are making a conscious decision not to marry," Dr. Hagestad added.

Yet economic concern is increasing, as more and more women stay single by choice. Once a woman never worried about whether or not to marry, only whom to marry. She was comfortable in the knowledge that other people would make the hard decisions for her and that she need not worry about her future.

Today I find economic fear a common characteristic of the single women I meet in my workshops. It is a fear that hits them much earlier than their married counterparts, who sometimes don't begin to think of their future security until they are in the 40–45 year range. This fear hits the single woman hardest at two stages:

- Around her 35th birthday and
- As she approaches retirement.

Take the case of Mary McAllister, an extremely bright and personable young woman from Anderson, Indiana, who dropped out of college to take a five-month "sojourn" in New York City—and finds herself still there fifteen years later "and broke."[4]

The biological breakpoint of her upcoming thirty-fifth birthday has made Mary stop and take stock. She is beginning to realize that she may never have anyone but herself to depend on. There just may not be a white knight in her crystal ball; and the time clock on having children is running out. Mary, who's filled her fifteen-year sojourn with a variety of stop-gap jobs, realizes she has not established strong professional credentials, and now finds herself competing in the job market with younger, more freshly educated women.

For the woman retiring today who has spent twenty-five to forty years with the same firm, the corporation has become father-husband source of security to her.

Retirement for these single women is probably more traumatic than retirement for any other group. Married men often have trouble adjusting to staying at home—and their wives have equal problems coping with their constant presence. But retirement for a single woman represents almost a cutting of her umbilical cord of emotional security. Her work has literally been her life. Once she's been given the gold watch, she finds she can't go back again. Though she may try to return to her place of employment to have lunch with her ex-colleagues, she soon finds her still-active friends have no real interest in her life as a retiree.

Unfortunately from a financial point of view, many single young women spend a good part of their paychecks pampering themselves. They treat themselves more freely to clothing, jewelry, makeup, and little extravagances.

If, instead, the smart single woman begins to put a value on herself and accumulate her assets systematically, she can secure her financial future—and in many ways she will have more independence and "security" than her married sisters who might have been subject to drastic personal economic changes through widowhood, divorce, or family responsibilities. If she marries later, she will still have built her independence and the foundation for interdependence in her family.

Many single women never plan how they will leave their assets to their beneficiaries—simply because they have believed society's widely held assumption that single women have nothing to leave to anyone anyway. But chances are they do have an estate—their own assets, group insurance benefits, funds inherited from relatives, and possessions of real or sentimental value they have accumulated. It is also particularly important for singles to understand how they are economically penalized by estate taxes, which place a higher tax rate on beneficiaries who are not husbands, children, parents, or grandparents.

As an example, in Illinois, the chart "Examples of Relationships and Exemptions" indicates that a "class 1" relationship (one of those listed above) is accorded a $20,000 tax exemption. But the exemption for a brother or sister is only $10,000. The exemption for aunts, uncles, cousins, nieces, and nephews is $500. And the exemption for a friend is only $100.

CHAPTER 21

The Merry Widow

One of the first things I had to set to rights was money. Money matters. It really does. It is right up there with love and security and identity. After Martin died, I used to wake up with my teeth clenched thinking, "You son of a bitch! You really screwed me! . . . You didn't love us enough to provide for our future. And now we're all alone. No husband. No father. No money."

—Lynn Caine
Widow[1]

WIDOWHOOD IS an absolute fact of life for all married couples.

There are over 10 million widows in our country today and *few are merry*—and even fewer are prepared for this crisis.

Of all the changes in a woman's life, none is as shocking as the loss of the man with whom she has shared and built her life. In fact, the death of a spouse is the most stressful situation any person has to face, according to Dr. Thomas Holmes, a University of Washington psychiatrist.[2]

Ironically, even in our highly educated and affluent society, few are prepared to face the drastic life changes that will take place emotionally, socially, and financially. Even more disturbing is the fact that few are fully prepared to come to your assistance at this time of need.

Unfortunately, we prefer to shut the subject from our minds. It is painful to discuss the loss of a spouse, being alone, making decisions alone. There is often fear and confusion associated with the subject of widowhood, so we would rather ignore it, hoping it will take care of itself. As a result, we have not learned to prepare ourselves properly for widowhood.

(One hopes this situation will change as more and more

men and women become aware of the importance of learning to cope with death during life. Many books and articles are now published on this subject, and some universities offer extension courses to help families prepare for death.)

But for the unprepared, particularly women, the loss of a spouse is compounded by other problems. She is often not only frightened and alone, but she may be making family and financial decisions for the first time in her life. Financial decisions, at any age, without prior training or experience can be terrifying.

I have had women clients who could not even write a check, who knew nothing of the family financial matters of banking, investments, insurance, taxes, real estate, pensions, laws, and other financial factors that would direct their lives.

My research and client files are filled with tragic situations brought on by the unprepared widow. But somehow, until it happens to you or your immediate family and you are forced into the situation, you never fully comprehend the human need behind the statistics. The statistics themselves are disturbing.

• Your chances are three in four of outliving your husband —by an average of 7.8 years.

• Widows represent 12.6 percent of the population. Some 2.4 million of these women are in the labor force, making up 6.9 percent of all workers.[3]

• The incidence of widowhood has increased 40 percent since 1950, and that percentage will increase in the future, as the burgeoning over-65 population continues to grow.

• The average age of today's widow is 56. While reentering the labor market at any age is difficult, imagine the economic and social problems faced by a 56-year-old widow, with no recent work experience.

I have found that the most vulnerable woman is the widow whose husband wanted to protect her from the "hard facts of life" and didn't want her to "think about such things."

How often I have heard: "What did we do wrong? My husband always took such good care of me. I just assumed I would be financially secure throughout my lifetime."

One can clearly see that preparing for life alone is of vital importance to all women. I have found that most of the tragic situations faced in widowhood could have been avoided if women had known how to plan properly before the crisis occurred.

But where can a woman go to learn how to prepare for widowhood?

Where Do You Begin?

Hopefully, you will be reading this before you are a widow. If you have kept up the checklist of your money sources, in Chapter 6, you will have no problem organizing the necessary documents when you are thrust into widowhood.

Often the only time a widow is prepared for her spouse's death is when there has been a long illness before death which makes her aware of the importance of financial planning. Otherwise, widowhood instantly thrusts you into financial decisions. You will be facing a myriad of details, questions, necessary documents, papers, new people and authorities to contact, wills, probate, federal and state laws, and new life planning.

In this atmosphere of shock and confusion, where do you begin? What assets will be immediately available to you? How long will it take before you can collect on the balance of your spouse's assets? When, where, and how do you obtain the assets and benefits in your spouse's name? In whose name are the assets held?

Begin with understanding all your possible money sources. Coordinate, list and organize all your money sources. And understand which of these money sources will end, which will begin, and which will continue. Review the Twenty-five Steps to Economic Planning in Chapter 6.

Searching Out and Applying for Benefits

Widows and heirs have lost thousands of dollars in benefits because they didn't know of existing insurance benefits, pension benefits, credit life insurance, association benefits, and many other existing benefits.

Thousands of unclaimed accounts in banks and savings and loans are advertised in the papers every year because the depositors did not tell their families about them.

Too often, important papers are scattered in several locations. Be sure to search files, desks, drawers, and other areas where papers might be kept. I recommend you establish a central location for all important papers. This will eliminate confusion, wasted time, additional expense, and loss of benefits.

The people involved will become very important to you, and you will find it extremely helpful if you know your spouse's professional advisors: lawyer; accountant; investment, insurance, and real estate advisor; banker and trust officer. These advisors will not only be helpful to you in organizing your benefits, but will be of great importance to you in your future financial planning. It is also advisable to be acquainted with your husband's business advisors and his business associates.

OBTAINING THE DEATH CERTIFICATE

You will need a copy of the death certificate to apply for most benefits. You can order additional copies from the funeral director or secure copies from the office of the Registrar of Vital Statistics.

PROBATE

Check with your attorney for the probate details in your state. Probate varies among states. Whether or not probate is necessary is usually based on a number of considerations including the nature and amount of assets of the deceased. Probate is normally completed within six months to a year, except for very large or complex assets.

The probate process:

- Accumulates all assets of the estate
- Pays estate bills
- Distributes the estate according to the will.

YOUR ATTORNEY

If you do not have an attorney, friends or relatives can usually recommend one. If not, phone your local bar association for recommendations.

The guidance of a lawyer at this time is important. A lawyer's functions will vary according to your individual situation and the laws of your specific state. Attorneys can be of help in many areas including:

- Probate proceedings
- Guidance with respect to existing funds, expenses, taxes, transferring titles, and various legal matters
- Creating trust funds
- Drawing up or changing your will
- Conserving and distributing your property.

Locating Important Papers

PERSONAL ECONOMICS: BANKS, SAVINGS AND
LOANS, CREDIT UNIONS

SAVINGS—Give your bankers the numbers of your current checking and savings accounts. They will tell you how much money you may have immediate access to, and when and how to obtain it, as well as what waivers are required.

CREDIT AND LOANS—Inquire about credit life insurance on any loans outstanding. Such insurance would pay off the debt.

I suggest you inquire about credit life insurance before paying any bills. Destroy all excess credit cards of the deceased and inform the issuing company of the death of the cardholder. (One widow seeking to establish her own credit found her dead husband had better credit than she did—so she kept his cards.)

SAFE DEPOSIT BOX—Check with your attorney or bank before opening your safe deposit box. In some instances it is necessary to have a witness present, usually a representative of the state inheritance tax body.

TRUST FUNDS—Contact your attorney and trust officer regarding existing trust accounts, and discuss new trusts that you might wish to establish.

INSURANCE BENEFITS—Do you understand the benefits and settlement options of your spouse's life insurance? Do you know if there are any loans against the policies or if the policies have been assigned to another party? (Many widows are shocked to find that there are large loans against their husband's insurance policies.)

You should change the beneficiary on any policies on which the deceased is named beneficiary. Most insurance benefits are paid within a few days, but delays could occur if death was accidental, or if death was within the contestable period of two years.

Be sure to review cancelled checks for any evidence of insurance payments on misplaced or unknown policies.

Many beneficiaries overlook little-known additional insurance benefits. Therefore be sure your policies answer the following questions:

• Do any policies cover accidental death benefits, if applicable?

• Are there any lapsed policies which, while premiums may not have been paid for some time, may still pay a benefit under the extended term provision?

• Are there any existing health policies which include a death benefit or medical reimbursement?

• Are any juvenile policies in effect on which the deceased is covered under the pay or death benefit? If so, premiums on the policy will be waived for a specific number of years (usually until the insured is 25).

• Do any policies contain a guaranteed purchase option advance purchase privilege that may be applicable? If no additional insurance has been purchased under the privilege during the purchase period (usually extending ninety days following marriage, birth, or adoption), the beneficiary may be eligible for the amount of the benefit which could have been purchased.

• If a lengthy period of illness preceded death, are any premiums returnable (under the disability waiver rider) which were made during this period?

• Do you have a family policy or family term insurance that provides for a paid-up term policy on the spouse and children?

• Are there any premium refunds due from premiums paid in advance?

Be sure also to notify the insurer carrying the deceased's homeowner's and auto insurance.

INVESTMENTS—Upon death, notify the deceased's stockbroker to freeze the account and nullify all brokerage instructions such as "stop orders" and "good till cancelled" orders.

BUSINESS ECONOMICS: EMPLOYEE BENEFITS

Many assumptions about fringe benefits lead to wasted and misunderstood benefits. Employees often assume that pension benefits will be paid to their spouse if death occurs before official retirement; this is seldom true. Many widows overlook benefits vested with former employers.

The U.S. Department of Labor's recently published booklet,

Often-Asked Questions about the Employee Retirement Income Security Act of 1974, explains the many factors involved in your company pension plan. The new Pension Reform Law (ERISA) also makes existing pension plans more uniform and allows employees not covered by a pension plan the opportunity to set aside up to $1,500 a year tax free for their retirement. (See Chapters 9 and 10 for more pension details.)

EMPLOYEE BENEFITS/SELF-EMPLOYED—Many wives of men in business for themselves do not realize that they might be responsible for the debts of the business upon their spouse's death, or do not understand what arrangements have been made for the continuation of the business upon death. The above-mentioned Pension Reform Law increases the amount allowable for tax-free retirement funds to $7,500 for the self-employed.

CIVIL SERVICE BENEFITS—The widow of a Civil Service employee may be eligible for certain benefits, based on her husband's total years of service and the highest average base salary earned during any three consecutive years of credit service. Contact the Civil Service office for information.

RAILROAD RETIREMENT BENEFITS—If the deceased was employed for ten years or more with a railroad, benefits would be provided by railroad retirement rather than Social Security. However, make the initial contact for railroad benefits through your local Social Security office.

GOVERNMENT ECONOMICS

SOCIAL SECURITY—Social Security benefits are based on "average monthly wage" in covered employment as determined by the Social Security office. Contact your local Social Security office for further information. See the Social Security chapter for a more comprehensive explanation.

See your Social Security office also to inquire about:

LUMP SUM BENEFIS—There is a lump sum death benefit with a maximum amount of $255.

MONTHLY INCOME BENEFITS—A monthly income is paid to a widow with children so long as the youngest dependent child is under 18. This income stops when there is no child under 18. (However, children who are full time students can continue to receive benefits until age 22.) If and when the widow has no eligible children, as above, no income benefits are paid until she reaches age 60. If benefits are taken at this age, they are on a reduced basis thereafter.

If the widow suffers a serious disability, she could be eligible for benefits at age 50.

Where income benefits are received, earned income can reduce or eliminate Social Security benefits.

VETERANS BENEFITS—For dependents of qualified veterans (those serving during designated periods of wartime as listed below), there may be a burial benefit of up to $400 and a monthly income death benefit. If death was service connected, the monthly income is standard according to military pay grade. If death was not service connected, the monthly income varies per dependents' current income. Contact your nearest Veterans' Administration office for details on monthly income death benefits.

General eligibility dates for benefits described above are as follows:

World War I—April 6, 1917, through November 11, 1918
World War II—December 7, 1941, through December 31, 1946
Korean War—June 27, 1950, through January 31, 1955
Viet Nam War—August 5, 1964, through May 7, 1975

TAXES—See chapter on laws and marriage and empty estates for tax laws applicable to your state. Consult your attorney and accountant for guidance.

CHAPTER 22

What is the Economic Status of Today's Woman?

Of course women are important . . . they control the wealth of the country.

—NELSON A. ROCKEFELLER

THIS STATEMENT was made with the traditional authority, half chuckle, and wide grin that always accompany this remark, when the Vice President appeared on a "Face the Nation" broadcast.

"Putting a value on the contributions of the homemaker would be as impossible as putting a value on the time I contribute to charity."[1] So said Robert Hill, a sensitive, knowledgeable attorney for the powerful House Ways and Means Committee, when I inquired about progress being made in measuring the value of the homemaker for various tax purposes.

"When we consider the working couple, let's eliminate the *unusual case* of the working wife and discuss the *typical case* of the working husband."[2] That statement came from Robert Tilove, pension expert and a senior vice president of a major actuarial firm. He was responding to reporters' questions on married couples' contributions to Social Security during a press conference held by the prestigious foundation that funded Mr. Tilove's new book on public employee pensions and Social Security.

These three statements tell us more about the status of women today than one sees at first glance.

They attest to the phenomenon that is taking place today:

For the first time in the history of our country, the wealthy, the powerful, the experts, and the prestigious are at least a decade behind the knowledge, information, awareness, and status changes of the women of this country.

Never before have the women of America played a more important role in the economic security of the family and the economic growth of this country, whether the "authorities" recognize this or not.

To understand the overwhelming changes in women's status, one must first examine the causes of these changes.

Never before have we seen such swift and sweeping changes affecting women in such a brief span of time. Never before have we had a more educated, informed, and self-confident society of women. Never before have we seen simultaneous revolutions occurring in *social attitudes, economics, communications, and legislation.*

The changing *social attitudes* of women are seen by their actions. There is a dramatic increase of women in general in the labor force, with a particular upsurge in working wives and women reentering the labor market after their children are in school or grown, or as a consequence of widowhood or divorce.

These attitude changes are evidenced too by women's increased educational attainments—more and more are getting college degrees; more and more are taking evening and daytime classes and extension courses at community colleges, high schools, and special training programs.

Further proof of these new attitudes can be seen in women's changing life-styles. Women are marrying later and having fewer children, preferring a combination of homemaking and career; they are living longer and raising their expectations and self-esteem.

Another factor has been the *economic* times in which we live. We are living in a time in history when the value of the dollar is fluctuating daily and eroding before our eyes and beyond our control. We now know that economic problems are not just for the old, the poor, or the fellow next door but that they might hit us with lightning swiftness whether or not we have the opportunity to prepare for them. Economic problems are now externalized and no longer hidden under the table; we talk about them, we share problems, experiences, and solutions as openly as we would discuss a new diet.

In *communications*, not only are the print and broadcast media covering these new changes meticulously, but women themselves have formed one of the most powerful and organized communication networks on a person-to-person basis through the many women's groups connected with their business, profession, community, school, church or political and special interest organizations. Today a new change affecting their lives flashes across this country faster than the speed of a telegram. Not only are women informed, but the breakfast, lunch, and dinner tables have become the center of this discussion for their friends and all members of the family to share.

Both state and federal *legislation* affecting women's economic lives is changing swiftly: whether the bills relate to credit, child care, child support, estate laws, family laws, probate, community property or separate property laws, they will have an impact on women's future economic lives. As of February 15, 1976, 130 bills affecting women were pending in the House of the 94th Congress; there are 19 bills on Social Security alone affecting women. In 1968 the state of California had five bills relating to women introduced into the legislature; in 1973 there were over 150.

To understand women's new importance in the economy, let us first measure her numbers in the accepted economic terms of population, production, consumption, and distribution.

Population

• 109.4 million women comprise 51.2 percent of the population.

• 78.1 million women are over 16 years of age.

• Women live longer—to 74.8 years, compared with 67 years for men.

• Voting population: 76.8 million women are 18 and over, or 52 percent of the total population over 18, reflecting the increased number of women living longer.

Production

• 37. 7 million women were in the labor force as of February 1976.

• 53 percent of all women 18 and over are in the labor force.

• Women represent 40 percent of the total work force.

• 58 percent of the female work force is married, contributing 25 to 40 percent of family income.

• 13.3 million single, widowed, and divorced women are in the labor force.

• From 1960 to 1970, as 9 million women increased their personal income through employment, the Gross National Product grew from $503 billion to $1,047 billion.

Consumption

• Married women purchase for and/or influence over 46 million households representing 164 million consumers, or 84 percent of the population. These families have an income of $626 billion, accounting for 81 percent of total personal income.

• 27.8 million single, widowed, and divorced women make consumer decisions.

• 6.8 million households are headed by women.

• One often overlooked area is the important role of the nation's 37.7 million working women in purchasing goods and services in the business world.

Distribution

In analyzing the distribution of women's wealth, mathematics and myths become confused. While statistics state that 5 million women have asset ownership of over $60,000, and there are supposedly 90,836 female millionaires, I am afraid I would have to question the purpose and reality of legal ownership versus management versus control versus non-control versus estate tax purposes.

Often women's ownership is an illusion, for assets are placed in women's names for tax purposes, but management and control remain in others' hands (usually husbands').

While there are, of course, a few Lady Bountifuls who marry or inherit large sums of money, if we are to measure the wealth of women by the enormous wealth of a limited few and not by all the women in our country, then we cannot put the statistics in proper perspective.

Other statistics give us evidence that large numbers of women have suffered extreme economic hardships because the distribution of wealth has left them struggling or at below-survival levels.

• Half of the women over 65 live on $2,000 a year.
• 16 percent of working wives have husbands with incomes under $7,000 a year.
• One-third of poverty families are headed by women.
• There has been an increase of 33 percent in female-headed families living in poverty in the last decade.
• Women's median income is only 57 percent of men's. (Men's median income is $12,152; women's median income is $6,957.)

Comparing the figures of distribution with those of consumption and production, it is hard to rationalize how women can have such collective economic power and still be left with little or no individual asset ownership. The consumer economy depends on women. The productive economy could not run without women. The money that runs this country flows through women's hands, yet only a minuscule amount winds up in their pocketbooks.

What blocks women's consumption and production strength from translating itself into distribution strength?

The answer to this question has been the goal of my research. While we discussed many of these economic blocks in this book, we have only begun to scratch the surface. But little by little, women throughout the country are finding the answers through diligent investigation.

The magnitude of women's role in the economy and consumer purchasing must be measured and understood. Married women are purchasing agents for over 46 million households with an income of $626 billion comprising 84 percent of the population, and 27.8 million single women make personal and family economic decisions. These 73.8 million women represent a position of great economic importance, responsibility, and impact on the national economy.[3]

A working wife has significant economic influence on her family's purchasing power, through her earned income from the labor market. Her contribution to the family's ability to pay for consumer and credit spending is growing annually. The Department of Labor's *1975 Handbook on Women Workers* shows that married women constitute 58 percent of the female labor force and many wives contribute 25 to 40 percent of the family's total resources.

One often overlooked area is the working woman's role in the purchase of goods and services in the business world. While she might not have fiduciary management responsibility, her impact on business decisions and office purchases is substantial. Who makes the airline reservations? The hotel reservations? The luncheon reservations? Who often purchases the supplies in the office? And who writes the office checks and deposits the money in the banks?

When I started my money manager workshops for women for a new bank opening in the heart of Century City in Los Angeles in September 1973, one of their goals was to establish a leadership position in the women's market, as there were 28,000 women spending their working hours in Century City. Their average income was just under $9,000. Hence, as a group they accounted for $250 million a year.⁴ In addition to this marketing potential, the bank found that many of the secretaries and/or women office managers decided where the business accounts would be deposited.

Even with the competing giant California branch banks in the Century City area, the First Los Angeles Bank celebrated its first year as the fastest-growing bank in the history of California banking. It opened its first year with $4 million in assets and closed it with $46 million in assets, and women making personal, family, and business decisions were an important part of that record growth.

Women, in fact, have become one of the important marketing segments in the banking industry primarily because individual consumers are of great importance to bankers today. The role of individuals as providers and users of funds is vital to the banking industry's success. The commercial banking industry doubled in size from 1963 to 1973, with individuals supplying $274 billion in deposits while business supplied only $33 billion. At the same time, 10 million women entered the labor market. Certainly these statistics are correlative.

The following chart illustrates how women's entrance into the labor and money markets has become a major force in banking, finance, and economics.

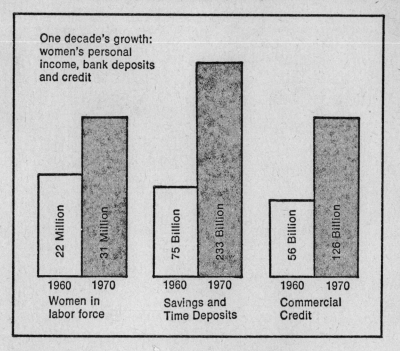

One decade's growth: women's personal income, bank deposits and credit

1960	1970
22 Million	31 Million

Women in labor force

1960	1970
75 Billion	233 Billion

Savings and Time Deposits

1960	1970
56 Billion	126 Billion

Commercial Credit

The impact of women on the economy is not only being felt, but measured, by women themselves, by business—and maybe someday even by the economists.

Most of our former laws and systems were based on society's attitude that women were supposed to be dependent. It was assumed they had neither the education nor knowledge to make valid decisions, and therefore had to be protected.

Today's woman has become an important and active economic contributor to the U.S. economy. Her goal is not to divide herself from other women or from the men with whom she has shared and built her life, be they husband, son, father, friend, or business associate. Today's woman's goals and desires are the same as they always were, to build a better life for herself and her family.

As this landmark Bicentennial year ends with Americans

moving into their third century of independence, the new frontier to conquer lies in the search for new ways to control and secure our economic destinies. Woman's continuing investigations into the systems that control our economic lives—and effecting changes within these systems—are charting the course Americans will take toward their Tricentennial.

The challenge is there, and women are taking the lead in meeting it. At times our economic progress seems slow. But, inexorably, women are moving forward. And we will never go back!

Notes

Chapter 1   Women's Economics: Is There a Difference?
1. Ernest R. Groves, *The American Woman: The Feminine Side of a Masculine Civilization* (1937).
2. Robert L. Heilbroner, *The Economic Problem* (Englewood Cliffs, N.J.: Prentice-Hall, 1970), p. 16.
3. John Kenneth Galbraith, *Economics and The Public Purpose* (Boston: Houghton Mifflin, 1973).

Chapter 2   Society of Enemies—or Partners?
1. Walter Hunt Blumenthal, *American Panorama* (Worcester, Mass.: A. J. St. Onge, 1963), p. 8.
2. Robert L. Heilbroner, *The Economic Problem* (Englewood Cliffs, N.J.: Prentice-Hall, 1970), p. 33.
3. Ernest Ludlow Bogart, *Economic History of the American People* (New York: Longmans, Green and Company, 1935), p. 12.
4. Scott Burns, *Home, Inc.* (New York: Doubleday, 1975), p. 3.
5. Scott Burns, *Home, Inc.* (New York: Doubleday, 1975), p. 81.
6. John Kenneth Galbraith, *Economics and The Public Purpose* (Boston: Houghton Mifflin, 1973).
7. Scott Burns, *Home, Inc.* (New York: Doubleday, 1975), p. 81.
8. Charlotte Perkins Gilman, *Women & Economics*, 4th edition (Boston: Small, Maynard and Company, 1910), p. 99.

Chapter 3 $1 + 1 = \frac{1}{2} =$ Dependency
1. Aristotle, "Politics," *The Basic Works of Aristotle*, Edited by Richard McKeon (New York: Random House, 1941), p. 1131.
2. Thomas Wiseman, *The Money Motive* (New York: Random House, 1974), p. 25.
3. Thomas Wiseman, *The Money Motive* (New York: Random House, 1974), p. 258.
4. Walter Hunt Blumenthal, *American Panorama* (Worcester, Mass.: A. J. St. Onge, 1963), p. 9.
5. Charlotte Perkins Gilman, *Women & Economics* (New York: Harper & Row, 1966), p. 169.

6. *Wall Street Journal*, "The Future Revised: The Family, Troubled by Change," March 18, 1976, p. 1.
7. Francis Squire Potter, *Women, Economics and the Ballot* (Youngstown, Ohio: Vindicator Press, 1909), pp. 4, 5.
8. Virginia Johnson, Personal interview, Boston, March 16, 1976.
9. *Wall Street Journal*, "The Future Revised: The Family, Troubled by Change," March 18, 1976, p. 1.

Chapter 4　　Psychology of Money: Where It All Begins
1. Thomas Wiseman, *The Money Motive* (New York: Random House, 1974), p. 4.
2. Michael Harrington, *The Other America* (Baltimore, Md.: Penguin Books, Inc., 1962), p. 17.
3. Thomas Wiseman, *The Money Motive* (New York: Random House, 1974), p. 267.

Chapter 5　　Time Is Money
1. Dee Dee Ahern, "Money Manager Workshop Handbook" (privately published, 1974).

Chapter 6　　Money at the Root: Your Money Sources
1. Robert L. Heilbroner, *The Economic Problem* (Englewood Cliffs, N.J.: Prentice-Hall, 1970), p. 8.
2. Aristotle, *Metaphysics X–XIV* (London: Loeb Classical Library, 1935), p. 340.
3. Dee Dee Ahern, *Economics of Being a Widow* (privately published, 1974), pp. 9–17.

Chapter 7　　The Money Stages in Your Life
1. Aristotle, *Metaphysics X–XIV* (London: Loeb Classical Library, 1935), p. 339.
2. Campbell R. McConnell, *Economics: Principles, Problems and Policies* (New York: McGraw Hill, 1972), p. 660.

Chapter 8　　Take It or Leave It: The Paycheck
1. Charlotte Perkins Gilman, *Women & Economics*, 4th ed. (New York: Harper & Row, 1910), p. 8.
2. Mary Elizabeth Pidgeon, *Women in the Economy of the U.S.* (Washington, D.C.: Women's Bureau, U.S. Department of Labor, 1937), p. 51.
3. Dee Dee Ahern, "The Economic Status (?) of Women" (privately published, 1973).

Chapter 9　　Their Money: The Private Pension System
1. Muriel F. Swift, *Chicago Tribune*, "At 77, the Golden Years Are Turning to Brass," March 1975.

2. *The Historic Development of the Private Pension System* (Washington, D.C.: Congressional Research Service, 1973).
3. *Women in Poverty* (Washington, D.C.: U.S. Commission on Civil Rights, June 1974), p. 43.
4. *The New York Times*, March 1976.
5. *Women in Poverty* (Washington, D.C.: U.S. Commission on Civil Rights, June 1974), p. 43.
6. David Hapgood, *The Screwing of the Average Man* (New York: Doubleday, 1975), p. 202.
7. *1975 Handbook on Women Workers* (Washington, D.C.: Women's Bureau, U.S. Department of Labor, 1976).
8. Walter Hunt Blumenthal, *American Panorama* (Worcester, Mass.: A. J. St. Onge, 1963), p. 23.
9. *Time*, "Americans On The Move," March 1976.
10. *1975 Handbook on Women Workers* (Washington, D.C.: Women's Bureau, U.S. Department of Labor, 1976), p. 19.

Chapter 10   Your Money: The Individual Retirement Act (IRA)

1. Warren Shore, *Social Security: The Fraud in Your Future* (New York: Macmillan, 1975), p. 139.
2. "Women in Poverty," (Washington, D.C.: U.S. Commission on Civil Rights, June 1974), p. 43.
3. Leonard Groupe, "Dollars and Sense," *Chicago Daily News*, 1975.

Chapter 11   Are Women on the Fringe of Benefits?

1. T. J. Gordon and R. E. Lebleu, "Employee Benefits, 1970 to 1975," *Harvard Business Review*, Jan.–Feb. 1970, pp. 93, 102.
2. Herbert S. Dennenberg, *Los Angeles Times*, "Women Aim Sights on 'Chauvinist' Insurers," 1975.
3. *Consumer View Newsletter*, "Women and Disability Benefits" (New York: First National City Bank, Feb. 1976), p. 3.
4. Susanne A. Stoiber, *Sex and the Nation's Insurance Industry* (Washington, D.C.: Committee for National Health Insurance, 1973).
5. Women Employed, Chicago, Illinois, Testimony and hearings of the Illinois Insurance Department regarding Rule 26:05, Feb. 3, 1976, p. 5.
6. *Chicago Tribune*, "Health Insurance—A 'Fringe' You Can Lose with Job," 1975.

Chapter 12   Public Employee Pension Funds (Federal, State and Local)

1. Robert Tilove, *Public Employee Pension Funds* (New York: Columbia University Press, 1976), p. 5.
2. *The Action Report IBEW Local 18*, vol. 2, April 1974.
3. *Barron's*, "Social Security. . . ," March 1976, p. 1.

Chapter 13   Who's Dependent on Whom? Social Security

1. Ella Polinsky, "The Position of Women in the Social Security System," *Social Security Bulletin* 32, no. 7, July 1969.
2. *Social Security Handbook*, publication 73–10135 (Washington, D.C.: U.S. Department of Health, Education and Welfare, 1974).
3. Arthur S. Flemming, Testimony before U.S. Senate Special Committee on Aging, 1975.
4. Tish Sommers, Testimony before U.S. Senate Special Committee on Aging, September 1975, p. 7.
5. Warren Shore, *Social Security: The Fraud in Your Future* (New York: Macmillan, 1975), p. 79.
6. *Historical Development of the Private Pension System* (Washington, D.C.: Congressional Research Service, March 24, 1972), p. 16.
7. Tish Sommers, Testimony before U.S. Senate Special Committee on Aging, September 1975, p. 5.
8. Alfred Allan Lewis, with Barrie Berns, *Three Out of Four Wives* (New York: Macmillan, 1975), p. 46.
9. Democratic Study Group, Task Force on Women, U.S. House of Representatives hearings on legislation affecting women, Feb. 15, 1976.

Chapter 14   Empty Estates

1. W. Ecker-Racz, *The Politics and Economy of State and Local Finance* (Englewood Cliffs, N.J.: Prentice-Hall, 1970), p. 65.
2. William E. Simon, Testimony before the House Ways and Means Committee on Estate Taxes, March 22, 1976.
3. Laura Lane, "Let's Get Rid of the Widow's Tax," *Farm Journal*, September 1975.
4. *Christian Science Monitor*, "Estate Tax Reform Would Aid Wealthy Most," April 1976.
5. *The Wall Street Journal*, "A New 'Soak-the-Rich' Theory," April 1976.

Chapter 15   The Expensive Guarantee: Insurance

1. Peter Shuck, Testimony before U.S. Senate Anti-Trust and Monopoly Judiciary Committee, February 23, 1973, p. 3.
2. Senator Philip A. Hart, Testimony before U.S. Senate Anti-Trust and Monopoly Judiciary Committee, February 20, 1973, p. 1.
3. *Selling To The Ladies*, 4th printing (Research and Review Service of America, 1971), p. 31.
4. A Sex Discrimination and Disability Income Insurance Plan, State of Illinois, July 1975, pp. 9–10.
5. Women Employed, Chicago, Illinois, "Sex Discrimination in Disability and Health Insurance," pp. 4–7.
6. John A. Durkin, Testimony before U.S. Senate Anti-Trust and Monopoly Judiciary Committee, February 22, 1973, p. 10.
7. *Boston University Law Review* 53, no. 3 (1973): 650.

8. Herbert S. Dennenberg, Testimony before U.S. Senate Anti-Trust and Monopoly Judiciary Committee, February 22, 1973, p. 3.
9. Herbert S. Dennenberg, *Shoppers' Guide to Life Insurance*, 1972.

Chapter 16   The Legal Pickpocket: Annuities
1. *Life Insurance Handbook*, 5th printing (New York: Life Insurance Institute, August 1972), p. 29.
2. Sylvia Porter, *Sylvia Porter's Money Book* (New York: Doubleday, 1975), p. 804.
3. *Life Insurance Handbook*, 5th printing (New York: Life Insurance Institute, August 1972), p. 28.
4. *Women in Poverty* (Washington, D.C.: U.S. Commission on Civil Rights, June 1974), p. 46.
5. *Boston University Law Review* 53, no. 3 (1973): 635.

Chapter 17   Giving Women Credit
1. William Moskoff, *Women and Credit in Illinois* (Springfield, Ill.: Sangamon State University, 1975), p. 5.
2. Jane Roberts Chapman, "Women's Access To Credit," *Challenge*, Jan.–Feb. 1975, p. 1.
3. *Purchase Influence: Measure of Husband/Wife Influence on Buying Decisions* (New Canaan, Conn.: Haley Overholser Associates, 1972), p. 2.
4. *1975 Handbook on Women Workers* (Washington, D.C.: Women's Bureau, U.S. Department of Labor, 1976), p. 17.
5. Jane Roberts Chapman, and Margaret J. Gates, Testimony before the Joint Economic Committee of the U.S. Congress on the economic problems of women, July 1973.
6. *1975 Handbook on Women Workers* (Washington, D.C.: Women's Bureau, U.S. Department of Labor, 1976), p. 382.
7. Dee Dee Ahern, "Woman's Growing Financial Awareness and Her Impact on the Credit World," address to American Bankers Association Credit Conference, March 1974.
8. *The Challenge Ahead In Banking* (Chicago: Booze, Allen, Hamilton, 1974).
9. *Business Week*, "The Debt Economy," October 12, 1974, p. 45.
10. John Kenneth Galbraith, *Economics and The Public Purpose* (Boston: Houghton Mifflin, 1973).
11. *Business Week*, "Women Win More Credit," July 12, 1974.

Chapter 18   Laws and Marriage
1. William J. Goode, "Social Change and Family Renewal," in *Families of the Future* (Iowa State Press, 1971).
2. Sidney M. Jourard, "Reinventing Marriage: The Perspective of a Psychologist," in *The Family in Search of a Future* (Meredith Corporation, 1970).

3. Anne K. Bingaman, *The Impact of ERA* (Washington, D.C.: International Women's Year Commission, 1976).
4. International Woman's Year Committee for the Homemaker, report of Martha Griffiths, August 26, 1975.

Chapter 19   The Spoils: Divorce
1. Tish Sommers, "The Compounding Impact of Age on Sex," *Civil Rights Digest*, Fall 1974, p. 8.
2. Beatrice Mullaney, *National Enquirer*, "I Blame Women's Lib for Soaring Divorce Rates," August 1975.
3. Tish Sommers, "The Compounding Impact of Age on Sex," *Civil Rights Digest*, Fall 1974, p. 9.
4. Martha Patton, "In Divorce Court, Equal Rights Are No Advantage to Women," *Chicago Tribune*, 1975.
5. *New York Times*, March 1976, p. 1.
6. Anne K. Bingaman, *The Impact of ERA* (Washington, D.C.: International Women's Year Commission, 1976).
7. Barbara R. Bergmann, "The Economics of Women's Liberation," *Annals of New York Academy of Sciences* 208, March 15, 1973, pp. 154–160.
8. Marian P. Winston, and Trude Forsher, *Non-Support of Legitimate Children by Affluent Fathers as a Cause of Poverty and Welfare Dependence* (Los Angeles, Calif.: Rand Corporation, 1972).

Chapter 20   "Truly" Single
1. *U.S. News and World Report*, "For Singles, Life Isn't All 'Swinging,' " December 8, 1975, p. 67.
2. *1975 Handbook of Women Workers* (Washington, D.C.: Women's Bureau, U.S. Department of Labor, 1976).
3. *The Wall Street Journal*, April 1976, p. 1.
4. Mary McAllister, Personal interview, March 1976.

Chapter 21   The Merry Widow
1. Lynn Caine, *Widow* (Boston: Little, Brown and Co., 1974), p. 151.
2. *Business Week*, March 1976.
3. *1975 Handbook of Women Workers* (Washington, D.C.: Women's Bureau, U.S. Department of Labor, 1976).

Chapter 22   What Is the Economic Status of Today's Woman?
1. Robert Hill, Personal interview, March 1976.
2. Robert Tilove, Press conference By Twentieth Century Fund Foundation, New York, March 1976.
3. *Purchase Influence: Measure of Husband/Wife Influence on Buying Decisions* (Haley Overholser Associates, 1972), p. 2.
4. *Los Angeles Herald*, "Shrewd Banker Woos Woman," September 1973.

Acknowledgments

All personal and professional growth begins with the combined interest, efforts, and cooperation of many people.

My sincere gratitude to the special people who helped make this book possible. They played varied roles in its birth—some were invaluable resource people; some were generous with research material; others contributed their time and knowledge to my workshops; others sponsored my workshops and lectures; and still others chronicled the progress of my research.

Government

MADALYN MIXER	Regional Director, Women's Bureau, U.S. Department of Labor
CARMEN MAYMI	Director of Women's Bureau, U.S. Department of Labor
MARGARET JOHNSON	Counsel, Commission on Civil Rights
LEE RICHARDSON	Former Director of Education and Finance, Office of Consumer Affairs

MERVYN DYMALLY	Lieutenant Governor, State of California
MARI GOLDMAN	Founder, California Joint Legal Equality Committee; Attorney
HALLIE TENNER	Chairperson, Mayor Bradley's Commission on the Status of Women
ELSA CARROW	Coordinator, Mayor Yorty's Committee for the Education of Senior Citizens

Education

JOAN COWAN	University of Chicago Extension
MARIA DEL DRAGO	University of California at Berkeley, Extension
SHIELA KUEHL	U.C.L.A. Women's Center
BRENDA EDDY	Instructor, Georgetown University
DR. BARBARA BERGMANN	Professor of Economics, University of Maryland
DR. DORIS H. CHASIN	Regional Director, Institute of International Education
JANE FULTZ	California State University at Northridge
MARIAN MARSHALL	Los Angeles Unified School District

Finance

JOSEPH DiGANGE	President, First Los Angeles Bank (Century City)
JAN NATARO	First Los Angeles Bank
PAT WYSKOCIL	First Los Angeles Bank
KENNETH OBRECHT	President, Hawthorne Bank (Wheaton, Illinois)
EUGENE CARTER	President, First State Bank and Trust of Park Ridge (Illinois)
KAY MAZUY	Shawmut Banks (Boston)
PAUL MANIFF	Shawmut Banks (Boston)
DON HUGHES	Shawmut Banks (Boston)

Phillip Donovan	United California Bank (Retired)
Richard Murphy	Wells Fargo Bank
Fern Larsen	Security Pacific Bank (Retired)
Chris Dokoff	First Bank of Whiting (Indiana)
Mary-Lynn Greely	Springfield Marine Bank (Illinois)
Dave Creel	First Ogden Group (Illinois)
Howard Johnson	President, Water Tower Bank (Chicago)
John VonThourtnot	President, First National Bank of Geneva (Illinois)
Charles Cederloff	Glendale Federal Savings (California)
Christine Gillis	E. F. Hutton

Women Leaders

Tish Sommers	Founder, Alliance for Displaced Homemakers
Jane Roberts Chapman	Center for Women's Policy Studies
Sonia McCullum and Ann Poag	E.R.A., Central (Chicago)
Jan Dunlap	Self Management Institute
Ann Sherwood	American Association of University Women
Geraldine Hadsell	Former Chairperson, Legislative Roundtable, Los Angeles Chamber of Commerce (Women's Division)
Carol Hochfelder	Attorney
Elizabeth Forsling Harris	President, *Working Women* Magazine
Trude Forsher	Writer, Producer, Los Angeles Human Relations Committee
Marian Winston	Research Editor, Rand Corporation
Judith Fleming	Affirmative Action Officer

Media—Journalists, Authors

Mert Gusweiller	*Los Angeles Herald-Examiner*
Leonard Groupe	*Chicago Daily News*; Attorney

Jo Ann Lublin	*Wall Street Journal*
Warren Shore	Journalist; Author, *Social Security: The Fraud in Your Future*
Lynn Caine	Publicist; Author, *Widow*
Victoria Billings	Editor, *Daily Breeze*; Author, *Womansbook*
Jack Webb	Copley News Service
Diane Loehrs	Former Producer, Metromedia

My special thanks to my beloved sons, Rick and Dan Ahern, and my brother, Ed Kelleher, for their encouragement to continue with my work when the financial and physical burdens seemed unbearable.

My thanks to Myrtle Wood, Mike Stern, Rozie Cohen, Margaret Cupp, and Dolores Gonzalez for their years of support—and to Barbara Cook for her hours of reports and correspondence.

And to my editor, Fred Honig, thank you for believing.

And especially my appreciation to the thousands of women who have attended my workshops throughout the country. I will never forget the concerns and hopes you have shared with me and the other women. Knowing each of you has been an invaluable experience.

Index

205